STERLING BIOGRAPHIES

Jacques Cousteau

A Life Under the Sea

Kathleen Olmstead

STERLING

New York / London
www.sterlingpublishing.com/kids

For D.

STERLING and the distinctive Sterling logo are registered trademarks of
Sterling Publishing Co., Inc.

Library of Congress Cataloging-in-Publication Data

Olmstead, Kathleen.
  Jacques Cousteau : a life under the sea / Kathleen Olmstead.
      p. cm. — (Sterling biographies)
    ISBN-13: 978-1-4027-4440-2
    ISBN-10: 1-4027-4440-4
  1. Cousteau, Jacques Yves—Juvenile literature. 2. Oceanographers—France—Biography—
Juvenile literature. I. Title.

GC30.C68O46 2008
551.46092—dc22
[B]
                                                                                        2007048195

10 9 8 7 6 5 4 3 2 1

Published by Sterling Publishing Co., Inc.
387 Park Avenue South, New York, NY 10016
© 2008 by Kathleen Olmstead
Distributed in Canada by Sterling Publishing
c/o Canadian Manda Group, 165 Dufferin Street
Toronto, Ontario, Canada M6K 3H6
Distributed in the United Kingdom by GMC Distribution Services
Castle Place, 166 High Street, Lewes, East Sussex, England BN7 1XU
Distributed in Australia by Capricorn Link (Australia) Pty. Ltd.
P.O. Box 704, Windsor, NSW 2756, Australia

Printed in China
All rights reserved

Sterling ISBN 978-1-4027-6058-7 (hardcover)
        ISBN 978-1-4027-4440-2 (paperback)

For information about custom editions, special sales, premium and
corporate purchases, please contact Sterling Special Sales
Department at 800-805-5489 or specialsales@sterlingpublishing.com.

Designed by Audrey Hawkins for Simonsays Design!
Image research by Larry Schwartz

Contents

Events in the Life of Jacques Cousteau

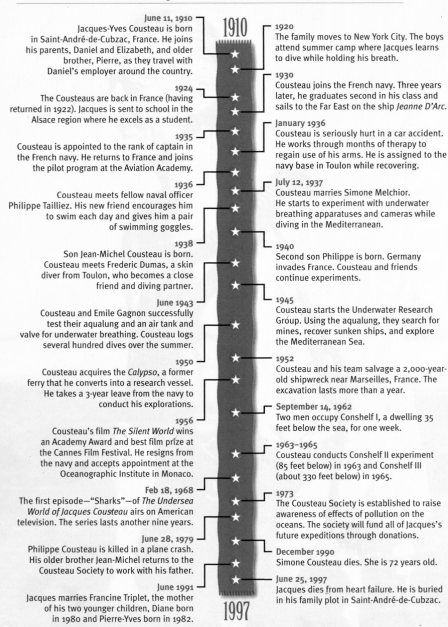

June 11, 1910
Jacques-Yves Cousteau is born in Saint-André-de-Cubzac, France. He joins his parents, Daniel and Elizabeth, and older brother, Pierre, as they travel with Daniel's employer around the country.

1920
The family moves to New York City. The boys attend summer camp where Jacques learns to dive while holding his breath.

1924
The Cousteaus are back in France (having returned in 1922). Jacques is sent to school in the Alsace region where he excels as a student.

1930
Cousteau joins the French navy. Three years later, he graduates second in his class and sails to the Far East on the ship *Jeanne D'Arc*.

1935
Cousteau is appointed to the rank of captain in the French navy. He returns to France and joins the pilot program at the Aviation Academy.

January 1936
Cousteau is seriously hurt in a car accident. He works through months of therapy to regain use of his arms. He is assigned to the navy base in Toulon while recovering.

1936
Cousteau meets fellow naval officer Philippe Tailliez. His new friend encourages him to swim each day and gives him a pair of swimming goggles.

July 12, 1937
Cousteau marries Simone Melchior. He starts to experiment with underwater breathing apparatuses and cameras while diving in the Mediterranean.

1938
Son Jean-Michel Cousteau is born. Cousteau meets Frederic Dumas, a skin diver from Toulon, who becomes a close friend and diving partner.

1940
Second son Philippe is born. Germany invades France. Cousteau and friends continue experiments.

June 1943
Cousteau and Emile Gagnon successfully test their aqualung and an air tank and valve for underwater breathing. Cousteau logs several hundred dives over the summer.

1945
Cousteau starts the Underwater Research Group. Using the aqualung, they search for mines, recover sunken ships, and explore the Mediterranean Sea.

1950
Cousteau acquires the *Calypso*, a former ferry that he converts into a research vessel. He takes a 3-year leave from the navy to conduct his explorations.

1952
Cousteau and his team salvage a 2,000-year-old shipwreck near Marseilles, France. The excavation lasts more than a year.

1956
Cousteau's film *The Silent World* wins an Academy Award and best film prize at the Cannes Film Festival. He resigns from the navy and accepts appointment at the Oceanographic Institute in Monaco.

September 14, 1962
Two men occupy Conshelf I, a dwelling 35 feet below the sea, for one week.

1963–1965
Cousteau conducts Conshelf II experiment (85 feet below) in 1963 and Conshelf III (about 330 feet below) in 1965.

Feb 18, 1968
The first episode—"Sharks"—of *The Undersea World of Jacques Cousteau* airs on American television. The series lasts another nine years.

1973
The Cousteau Society is established to raise awareness of effects of pollution on the oceans. The society will fund all of Jacques's future expeditions through donations.

June 28, 1979
Philippe Cousteau is killed in a plane crash. His older brother Jean-Michel returns to the Cousteau Society to work with his father.

December 1990
Simone Cousteau dies. She is 72 years old.

June 1991
Jacques marries Francine Triplet, the mother of his two younger children, Diane born in 1980 and Pierre-Yves born in 1982.

June 25, 1997
Jacques dies from heart failure. He is buried in his family plot in Saint-André-de-Cubzac.

A Life Under the Water

We enrich our souls when we reach out to enrich the souls of others.

It looked like any other dinner party. Friends were gathered around a table enjoying a good meal, celebrating the twenty-sixth wedding anniversary of Jacques and Simone Cousteau. There was cake for dessert, and everyone toasted the happy couple.

Jacques, turning to a large window near the table, raised his glass to toast the schools of fish swimming past. This was no ordinary party. They were thirty-five feet under the sea, safe and dry in Conshelf II, a research station designed and built by Jacques Cousteau.

Cousteau spent most of his life exploring oceans and sharing his discoveries with the world. He made it possible for people to experience the undersea world in a new way. Through his television shows, books, and movies, Cousteau brought the marine world into people's living rooms. His inventions actually changed the way people moved through the water. The aqualung allowed humans to breathe underwater and swim like a fish, while the diving saucer became a personal mini-sized submarine.

This thin Frenchman—usually wearing a red knit cap and standing on the bow of a ship—was a recognized symbol of exploration, adventure, and undersea life. Once Cousteau glimpsed the beauty of the underwater world, nothing was the same again.

CHAPTER 1

The Birth of an Explorer

It happened to me that summer's day . . . when my eyes opened to the world beneath the surface of the sea.

In the year 1910, Daniel Cousteau and his wife Elizabeth returned to their hometown of Saint-André-de-Cubzac on the west coast of France, in anticipation of the birth of their second child. Their first son, Pierre, was traveling with them. **M.** Cousteau, a lawyer, worked for James Hyde, an American businessman living in France. The Cousteaus traveled with Mr. Hyde, living in hotel rooms and on trains. It was an unusual life for a young family, but they all enjoyed the adventure. However, for now, they wanted to be close to home.

A recent photograph of Saint-André-de-Cubzac captures the quiet coastal town in France where Jacques-Yves Cousteau was born. Both of his parents were also born there, and their families still live in the area.

They returned to the small coastal town, which had a population of only 4,000, just in time. On June 10, 1911, they welcomed Jacques-Yves Cousteau into the family. The Cousteaus did not rest for long and Jacques—or Zheek, as his family called him—soon joined them on the road. Jacques, it would seem, was a traveler and explorer from the day he was born.

In Poor Health as a Child

Although Jacques was a plump and healthy baby, he was quite sick as a boy. He suffered from anemia—a disease caused by a lack of oxygen in the blood system—and stomach troubles. His doctors ordered bed rest. So, while his older brother Pierre could play with friends and enjoy the outdoors, young Jacques spent a great deal of time in the family's hotel rooms.

He was rarely lonely, though. Jacques entertained himself with books. He liked adventure stories best, in particular, "Henri de Montfreid's books about pearl divers, pirates, slaves, and smugglers." He also enjoyed James Fenimore Cooper's stories

about the American frontier and the fantasy stories of Jules Verne. These books were filled with action and adventure—things that a sick boy in bed could only imagine.

Exercising for Health

In 1918, Daniel took a new job with another wealthy American businessman. Eugene Higgins, much

As a child, young Cousteau enjoyed reading adventure stories such as James Fenimore Cooper's *The Last of the Mohicans*. An illustration from a 1910 edition is shown.

like James Hyde, moved often, and he wanted his lawyer to travel with him. Higgins was a robust man who enjoyed sports and outdoor activities. He insisted that Daniel join him in games

Jules Verne (1828–1905)

Jules Verne, a French novelist, is known as one of the "fathers of science fiction." He wrote about outer space, traveling to the center of Earth, flying around the world in a hot air balloon, and underwater adventures.

One of his most famous books—*20,000 Leagues Under the Sea* (1870)—is the story of Captain Nemo and his fantastic submarine, the *Nautilus*. Unlike the submarines of Verne's day, the *Nautilus* was comfortable and luxurious. There was a library, laboratory, and dining room, as well as comfortable quarters for all the men. Powered by electricity (before electricity was in common

This illustration from the 1870 edition of *20,000 Leagues Under the Sea* shows Captain Nemo on top of his submarine the *Nautilus*.

use), the submarine sailed through the seven seas battling giant squids, whales, and whirlpools. The crew gathered food from the ocean and distilled seawater for drinking. This story was so popular that the *Nautilus* and Captain Nemo were resurrected in a later novel, *The Mysterious Island*.

Since his death, Verne's popularity has grown as his novels have been translated into dozens of languages, turned into movies, and are still read by children the world over.

of tennis and golf, and the elder Cousteau rushed to keep up with his energetic employer.

Higgins believed that everyone needed plenty of exercise and fresh air. He was certain that Jacques, skinny and pale from so many years stuck inside a room or his bed, would benefit from physical activity. Higgins decided that swimming was the perfect solution.

Despite the doctor's orders that Jacques should avoid physical exertion, his parents agreed to Higgins's plan. Higgins took Jacques down to the water and taught the boy to swim. As it turns out, Jacques loved the water. For a boy who spent so much time in bed, swimming and floating through the water felt like pure freedom.

In 1920, when Jacques was ten years old, Higgins went back to New York City, with the Cousteaus right behind. They moved into an apartment on the upper west side of Manhattan and quickly settled into their new home.

After moving to New York City, Jacques and Pierre learned to play American city games like the children shown in this c. 1910 photograph playing stickball—a form of baseball played with broom handles instead of bats.

Jacques and his older brother Pierre fit easily into life in America. It was not long before they were playing baseball in the streets and speaking fluent English. They attended a public school in the area and even went to summer camp in Vermont.

Underwater for the First Time

It was exciting being in the Vermont countryside for a change. The Cousteau boys were so used to city life that it was nice to play among the trees for a while. Their camp was on Lake Harvey and there was a long dock leading into the water. However, the campers were not allowed to jump off this dock because there was a pile of sticks and branches resting on the lake bottom. Anyone jumping from the dock could get hurt.

One of the camp counselors, Mr. Boetz, gave young Jacques the task of clearing these branches. According to Jacques, he and the counselor did not get along and this was Mr. Boetz's way of punishing him.

It was in the waters of Lake Harvey, Vermont—seen here in a recent photograph—that Cousteau attended summer camp and learned to swim underwater by holding his breath.

Approaching the end of the dock, Jacques slipped into the deep water, filled his lungs with air, and dipped below the surface of the lake. It was his first time underwater. Jacques began to kick his feet and wave his arms until he found himself at the bottom of the lake. He grabbed one branch and dragged it back up. He handed the piece of wood to a friend and went back down for more. Jacques dived over and over again until all the branches were on land and the area was safe for diving.

Jacques's underwater experience was the first of many life-changing experiences. He later admitted that the branch-clearing job was very hard work, but it had a great benefit: "Diving in that murk without goggles, without a mask . . . that's where I learned to dive." It was an experience that he often recalled as an adult. It taught him a great deal about his own strength and what could be done when you are determined. "I spent two or three weeks diving into that lake and eventually I learned how to hold my breath underwater," he said.

Returning to France

Two years later, the Cousteau family was back in France. Jacques went to school but was not a good student. His parents knew he was a smart boy but worried that Jacques lacked discipline when it came to his studies. However, whenever he was excited about something specific, he worked happily away until it was finished. He was always building things, taking machines apart and putting them back together again, but when it came to schoolwork, he seemed to quickly lose interest.

One day, Jacques, insisting that a rock thrown at high speed would leave only a small hole in the glass, broke all the windows at his school. This act of vandalism—or as Jacques might have considered it, a physics experiment—resulted in

Jacques being expelled from school. His parents decided that Jacques needed a change.

He was sent away to military school at the age of fourteen. His school was in the Alsace region of France near the German border. It was a strict school with an emphasis on discipline and grades. Surprisingly, Jacques enjoyed his time there and flourished as a student. He started to do very well in school and was eager to learn more.

It was during this time that Jacques developed an interest in film. "I created at school a film production company. I acquired a small 9.5 mm camera and I started making films." Using this camera, he started to write and direct his own films. Jacques usually cast himself in the lead role, often as the villain rather than hero. Years later, Jacques admitted that he enjoyed taking the camera apart and reassembling it just as much as he liked making the films. "I was fascinated by the hardware," Cousteau said. "That's how I got started—the camera, how to process the film and devise chemicals."

As a teenager, Cousteau used a 9.5 mm camera—like the one shown here—to make movies. It was a small, handheld camera, perfect for a young filmmaker.

Join the Navy and See the World

In 1930, after he had finished high school, Jacques Cousteau entered the French Naval Academy. He graduated three years later with the second-highest marks in his class. It was hard to believe this was the same boy who broke all the windows in his school! He was appointed to the rank of lieutenant and set sail on the *Jeanne D'Arc*, a naval training ship. They were heading to Asia—first to Singapore and Hong Kong—and then beyond.

Cousteau hoped he would see the whole world. He took his camera with him and made short films as he traveled aboard the *Jeanne D'Arc*. He captured dancers in Cambodia and Bali, street festivals in Viet Nam, and **geishas** in Japan. When the ship arrived in California, Cousteau visited Hollywood and shot film of movie stars such as Claudette Colbert and Douglas Fairbanks.

After his **tour** on the *Jeanne D'Arc*, Cousteau was stationed in Shanghai, China. One day, while on a ship traveling along the coast, he saw something extraordinary. "At Cam Ranh Bay in **Indochina**, at the hottest time of day, between noon and two o'clock, I saw people diving from their boats and then surfacing with fish in their hands." This image of men diving with such ease stayed with the young sailor. Even late in life, Cousteau would mention this incident in interviews as one of his inspirations to journey under water.

This picture of the *Jeanne D'Arc*, a French navy ship docked in New York Harbor, was taken in May 1934 during Cousteau's tour on the ship.

Cousteau was very fond of life at sea. He liked the travel and enjoyed working in the salty air, but he had other ideas for his career. He always craved adventure and excitement, and Cousteau thought flying could provide all that he needed. He would become a pilot and could already see himself sailing through the blue sky. Cousteau was certain that this was the place for him.

The young adventurer returned to France to enter the pilot program at the French Naval Academy. He was promoted to captain just before leaving the East. It was an exciting time for Jacques. He loved flying and was looking forward to a life as a pilot. Then, just before his final exams, disaster struck.

Life Changes in an Instant

Early in 1936, not long before graduating from the aviation academy, Cousteau was in a terrible car accident in France's Vosges Mountains. He was on his way to a friend's wedding when his car flipped over, and he was seriously injured. He spent a long time in the hospital with cracked ribs, two broken arms, and a crushed lung. When his left arm, already broken in five places, became infected, the doctors considered amputation. Jacques would not allow it. They were able to cure the infection, but his arm was paralyzed.

This was terrible news, but Jacques was determined to get better. Even though the aviation academy told him his career as a pilot was over, he refused to give up. It would take a lot of hard work but Cousteau knew he could regain full use of his arms. He overcame sickness as a child through exercise, and he would do the same again.

After eight months of physical therapy, Cousteau was able to move his fingers on his left hand only slightly, but he was encouraged by these results. He was on the road to recovery.

While recuperating in Toulon from his injuries, Cousteau met Philippe Tailliez. Toulon is now a popular resort town located on the French Riviera, along the southern coast of France.

Cousteau was sent to the navy base in Toulon, a small city on the southern coast of France. He was still weak from his injuries but could move both his arms again. While in Toulon, Jacques met another navy officer, Philippe Tailliez. They hit it off immediately and became fast friends. Philippe, who was an avid swimmer, encouraged Jacques to exercise in the water. He said it would help to strengthen his arms.

Restored to Health

Cousteau took his new friend's advice and went for daily swims in the ocean. At first, it was difficult to raise and lower his arms repeatedly, but soon he was gliding through the water, moving his limbs with ease. It was a wonderful day for Jacques when he felt his strength return. The ocean had restored him. As Cousteau has said, "Water is an embracing medium."

The ocean had restored him.

One day, Tailliez gave Cousteau a present. It was a pair of goggles to wear while swimming. The goggles, used by Polynesian and Japanese divers, protected a swimmer's eyes from the ocean's salt water. Tailliez told his friend that he would be able to open his eyes while underwater.

Philippe Tailliez (1905–2002)

Philippe Tailliez was born in Brittany, on the north coast of France. Even as a young boy, he was fascinated by the sea and water. He was athletic and curious, spending much of his time swimming, eventually becoming a champion in the sport. He joined the French navy in 1924 and met Jacques-Yves Cousteau when they were both stationed on the freighter *Condorcet* in Toulon.

Tailliez, like his father, was a career navy man. Philippe was well known outside naval circles, thanks to his long friendship with Cousteau. He worked alongside his friend while Cousteau pioneered both deep-sea diving and underwater filmmaking.

Tailliez wrote several books about their adventures on and below the seas. *To Hidden Depths*, published in 1954, is considered one of the first books to cover the history of deep-sea diving. His later books covered his own adventures as a diver searching for boats and treasures.

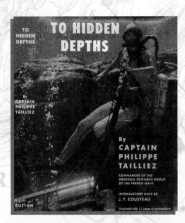

Shown is the first edition cover of Philippe Tailliez's *To Hidden Depths*. He worked closely with Cousteau for many years.

Tailliez stopped working with Cousteau in the early 1950s as Cousteau took on more work outside his naval duties. For the remainder of his life, Tailliez lived in the Toulon area.

Cousteau did not know that this simple gift would change his life forever. He put the goggles on and saw an entirely new world. Under the sea, Jacques found a world of color and life. The ocean floor was covered with bright green plants swaying in the currents. Schools of fish—blues, reds, yellows, oranges—swam past him. The water was perfectly clear. He could see all around him—in every direction—for what seemed like hundreds of feet. "The sand sloped down into a clear blue infinity. The sun struck so brightly I had to squint," he later wrote.

The awe-struck swimmer had never seen any scene like it before, and it changed him forever. "It happened to me that summer's day," Cousteau would later recall, "when my eyes were opened on the sea." He knew that he needed to be a part of it.

A 1990 photograph showing the undersea world of the Mediterranean. Cousteau probably saw the same bright colors when he first swam underwater wearing goggles.

CHAPTER 2

Struggles and Success

It fascinated me to do something that seemed impossible.

In 1936, while Cousteau was still recovering from his car accident, he went to visit his parents in Paris. At a party one night, he met a beautiful young woman named Simone Melchior. Jacques was twenty-six years old and Simone was seventeen.

She was confident and smart, and Jacques was immediately drawn to her. Her father, a retired navy admiral, was the director of Air Liquide—a company that was a leading producer of industrial gases for factories. Her father's work took his family all over the world, so Simone was already well traveled when Jacques met her. She had even lived in Japan for a few years when she was a girl.

Simone was still in high school, but Jacques visited her in Paris whenever he could. They continued their long-distance romance until Simone graduated. Then, on July 12, 1937, they were married. She returned to Toulon with Cousteau, and they settled into married life together.

Jacques and Simone married in 1937. They are shown here dressed up for a party in 1954.

Simone understood the life of a navy wife. Her mother and both grandmothers were married to navy admirals. She expected a home near the navy base and a husband who might travel a lot. As an officer's wife, she expected a life of formal dinners and special occasions. However, Simone suspected that Jacques was not a typical navy man. He had already lived a life of adventure, and she had no reason to expect that to change.

Cousteau's navy work—training new recruits on the base—allowed enough free time to dive. Simone often joined him in the water. She put on her own pair of goggles and explored with her husband and Philippe Tailliez. During their many years together—and Cousteau's many adventures in front of the camera—Simone remained at his side.

Skin Diving with Friends

As Toulon was a seaside town, many of the residents fished to earn a living. Some used boats to find their prey while others would dive underwater to catch the fish. These spear anglers, or skin divers, held their breath and dived to great depths to hunt for fish. One of these skin divers, Frederic Dumas, became another of Cousteau's closest friends.

Born in 1913, Dumas was raised on the French Riviera near Toulon. When Tailliez introduced him to Cousteau in 1938, Dumas was a champion spear diver with a great deal of experience in the waters near Toulon. Didi, as his friends called him, joined the unofficial team of Cousteau and Tailliez as they dived and explored in the ocean surrounding them.

Even as early as 1937, Cousteau was already experimenting with underwater breathing techniques. He was not the first person to think about life under water. When Dumas joined their diving group, they began to seriously explore ways that

Spear Fishing

Spear fishing required very little equipment. This 1979 photograph shows a boy spear fishing in Panama using only a mask and spear.

The simplest definition of spear fishing is, quite simply, catching fish with a spear. The advantage is that the only equipment needed is a spear—a sharpened stick or rod. When spear fishing, the diver can hunt underwater, or he can stab at the fish from shore or a boat.

In many areas, especially the Mediterranean in the 1930s when Cousteau first met Dumas, spear fishing was considered more than a means to find food. It was a competitive sport. Rules and regulations may have varied depending on the region, but a champion in the sport was determined by the size and number of fish caught in a specified time and how deep the spear diver ventured to catch the fish. No underwater-breathing apparatus was used. Goggles and swimming fins worn on the feet to increase speed were the only swimming aids used by these skin divers.

Modern day skin divers may use a variety of new equipment, including spear guns and air tanks.

would allow a swimmer to breathe underwater and still have freedom of movement.

Skin diving allowed freedom of movement but Cousteau could stay under only as long as he could hold his breath. It was difficult to explore if he had to return to the surface for air every few moments. At that time, there was a metal diving suit and helmet (called an atmospheric diving suit) that a diver could use and stay under for hours at a time, but the air hose for the suit was attached to a pump on land or onboard a boat, thus keeping the diver from roaming too far. Cousteau wanted to find a way that provided air like a diving suit but the freedom of skin diving.

It was difficult to explore if he had to return to the surface for air every few moments.

Underwater Devices from the Past

In his search for a practical underwater-breathing mechanism, Cousteau probably heard the stories of underwater journeys that had been told for thousands of years. There were tales of men in ancient Greece and Rome who used reeds or other hollow plants to breathe while under water. Drawings from ancient Assyria, near modern-day Iraq, depicted swimmers carrying bags through water. Although no one can say for certain, one theory supposed that these bags were used to provide air when underwater. In 400 **BCE**, Aristotle, a Greek philosopher, wrote about men going under in **diving bells**. There was even a story about Alexander the Great, a Macedonian king born in 356 BCE, who descended into deep waters while in a glass box. These were all wonderful stories, but Cousteau would need more practical and accessible solutions to breathing underwater.

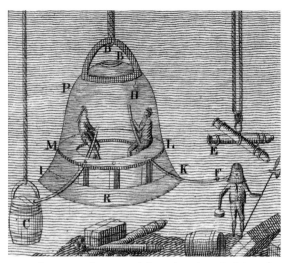

A 1728 illustration of a proposed design for a diving bell shows two men inside while a third explores the ocean floor. Air is supplied through hoses from a barrel suspended beside the bell.

Breathing Underwater

At first, Cousteau tried building his own air-supply system. He used a tank of oxygen with a rubber hose attachment for airflow. He strapped the tank onto his back and put a weight belt around his waist. Tanks of air can be buoyant and pull a diver to the surface. By wearing small weights in a belt, the diver can better control the depth of the dive. To keep warm when the water was cold, Cousteau wore a rubber suit of his own design. It was skintight and covered him from head to toe.

At first, Cousteau tried building his own air-supply system.

To test his new tank design, Cousteau donned his swimming equipment and dived underwater. The oxygen tank worked well for a while, but when he swam down to a depth of forty-five

The Atmospheric Diving Suit (ADS)

Even when not in use, the atmospheric diving suit looks like a large robot or something that an astronaut might wear. Air is supplied through a hose from a pump on shore or a ship. The diver wears a large metal helmet, usually round, with a glass front. Exhaled air escapes through a vent into the surrounding water.

Cousteau knew these suits well. The first one was invented in the 1700s, and many designs followed it. They were often used in shipbuilding as well as for building and repairing bridges. Also, if anyone wanted to walk along the ocean floor or examine a sunken ship, a diving suit was used.

Although it looks somewhat dated, the diving suit is still in use today. It is doubtful that anyone would wear the suit for a recreational dive to look at fish and coral, but it is still used by the navy and shipbuilders. The suit provides more protection for tough jobs that require large pieces of equipment. The diver can stay underwater longer than a worker using an air tank that has enough air for only a couple of hours. The diving suit allows the worker to stay underwater two or three times that length of time.

Atmospheric diving suits were bulky and cumbersome. Two men in diving suits stand by an air pump in this late-19th-century photograph. A rope is tied around their waists to keep them close to shore.

feet, he ran into trouble. Lost in his enjoyment of swimming and breathing underwater, Cousteau was following a fish when suddenly his spine bent backward. He was stopped short and in great pain. His eyes started to roll to the back of his head, and he became confused and dizzy. He found it difficult to move his limbs. Luckily, he managed to take off his weighted belt before passing out as he floated to the surface.

Cousteau wondered if there was a problem with the hose to his oxygen tank. Maybe his filter was not working properly. Because he was descending at the time, he might have suffered from nitrogen narcosis, a condition Cousteau referred to as "rapture of the deep," but the symptoms were more like decompression sickness, also known as the "bends."

In the end, Cousteau realized that he would have to abandon the idea of pure oxygen in his air tank as it became toxic if a diver went below thirty feet. Oxygen has a very adverse reaction to water pressure. Cousteau understood that a great deal of work still lay before him.

A World at War

Jacques and Simone's family quickly grew. Their first son Jean-Michel was born in 1938 and then a second son named Philippe in 1940. Together they had a very happy home. Friends visited often, and their house was filled with laughter and excited conversations—often about the ocean and diving. Jacques and his friends never tired of discussing plans to explore the underwater world and the possibilities for a workable underwater breathing device.

This domestic bliss was not reflected in the world around them, however. By the time Philippe was born, most of the Western world was involved in World War II.

Rapture of the Deep and the Bends

There are two great dangers that divers using air tanks face. Nitrogen narcosis, the condition that Cousteau refers to as the "rapture of the deep," may occur as a diver descends deeper and nitrogen gases build up in the blood stream. It produces an effect much like alcohol intoxication. The divers may become confused and disoriented. It is difficult to control their body and movements can become erratic. Divers may lose the ability to make decisions and even consciousness. Cousteau has said that he was more susceptible than others to this "rapture."

As divers return to the surface, they must be careful as well. The longer or deeper the dive, the more slowly they must ascend, so their body has a chance to release all of the nitrogen trapped in their bloodstream at a natural rate. If a diver ascends too quickly, a condition known as decompression sickness or "the bends" may occur, causing severe pain that may last for weeks—especially in the joints— momentary paralysis and sometimes death. The name—the bends—is derived from the body's reaction to the overload of nitrogen in the bloodstream. Afflicted divers often contort and bend involuntarily, and their joints may become swollen. The bends can occur anywhere, when there is a drastic and sometimes sudden change in pressure, including when one is in an underground mine or an airplane.

Divers must be careful while descending in the water. They control their speed by kicking their diving fins, or flippers, at a slow and steady pace.

In 1939, World War II began when Germany invaded Poland. Other countries took sides in the conflict and soon all of Europe was at war. England, France, Canada, and others joined forces to fight against Germany and Italy. No one knew how long the war would last and everyone was prepared for the worst.

Then, in 1940, Germany and Italy invaded France. Like many of his compatriots, Cousteau fought against these armies, and he took up his naval post operating the guns on one of the boats. However, it was a losing battle. In June of that year, France signed an agreement with Germany to stop the fighting in its country. For the next four years, the German army controlled France.

Following their recent occupation of France, German soldiers are photographed with bicycles, parading past the Arc de Triomphe in Paris, France, in 1940.

Life during wartime is always hard, but it was especially difficult for many of the French people. They were living with the enemy right next door. The invading armies took control of France's resources and food supplies. No longer could Simone simply walk to the store to buy a loaf of bread. She would need a coupon to stand in a long line for the bread, and even then, she might not receive anything. The German armies policed the areas with an iron fist. Anyone suspected of working against them or the Italian armies was quickly thrown in jail. Even without the daily explosions and gunfire associated with war, it was a dangerous time for French citizens.

Throughout the war, Jacques, Simone, and their two boys lived an exotic existence. The French navy was no longer active because of the **occupation**, so there was little work for Jacques to do. He was still receiving a small pay, and he supplemented the family's food rations with riches from the sea. Without real work, Cousteau and his friends found the time to continue their underwater experiments. So, while he was experiencing the wonders of the ocean and gathering food for his family and friends, "above water was occupied, ill-fed France."

Without real work, Cousteau and his friends found the time to continue their underwater experiments.

CHAPTER 3

In Occupied France

*When a person takes his first dive, he is born to
another world.*

It was 1943 and World War II was raging through
Europe. German and Italian forces continued to occupy
France, and Cousteau, Dumas, and Tailliez were still hard
at work beneath the ocean waves.

At that time, the German army knew there were
groups of people—known as the French Resistance—who
were working in secret against the Germans, so they kept
a close eye on the French people. This was also true in
Toulon. They kept close tabs on the town's citizens, but
fortunately, they ignored Cousteau and his team. "The
Germans considered me a harmless nut," he explained in
a 1972 interview. "And I did all I could to reinforce the
impression. I dived in the worst weather, and used the
excuse that I was spear fishing to help out the slender
rations we were allowed."

The activities of Cousteau and his crew must have
looked odd to any observer. Men in strange bathing suits
were going in and out of the water with tanks of air and
rubber hoses. They wore masks and had flippers on their
feet. They carried rubber hoses, and sometimes **snorkels**,
and movie cameras, but no one bothered them.

If the Germans had realized Cousteau was attempting
to build a personalized air tank and mask, they certainly
would have been interested. An underwater breathing

apparatus would be extraordinarily useful to any army—especially during a war. If they had watched him more closely, they would have seen that Cousteau was very close to success.

The French Resistance

Many groups made up the French Resistance during the Second World War. These groups consisted of men and women who worked in secret against the German and Italian armies ruling France. Some of these groups worked independently—especially those living in the countryside with little access to other groups—and others who belonged to a larger, more organized community. Spies for the Resistance were able to pass information about German and Italian plans and movement of troops. Even though they were trapped in their occupied country, resistance members were still an invaluable force when fighting the war.

As seen in this c. 1944 photograph, the French Resistance was made up largely of ordinary citizens fighting against the German occupation. It required great secrecy and was often fought from their own homes.

The French Legion of Honor, established by Napoleon Bonaparte, is France's highest honor offered to civilians and members of the military. Cousteau received the medal for his work with the French Resistance.

Although Cousteau did not like to discuss his work with the French Resistance during the war, at least one story of his bravery survives. Apparently, Cousteau stole an Italian officer's uniform, and while wearing this disguise, snuck into their headquarters, where he photographed secret documents. This information was then passed on to the **Allied forces**. In later years, Cousteau tried to downplay his Resistance work. The French government, however, thought differently. After the war, they awarded him the Legion of Honor, one of France's highest honors for his bravery.

The Mystery of Light and Water

From the time of his first dive with the goggles in 1936, Cousteau searched for ways to bring a camera into the water. He wanted to show people the wonderful new world he had discovered.

Cousteau knew that this was possible. In 1892, Louis Boutan, a French zoologist, began experimenting with underwater photography. His still photos were less than perfect—many of them were blurry and dark—but it was possible. Boutan published a book called *Undersea Photography* in 1900, and it was a favorite of Cousteau's.

The first, and most obvious question was how to keep the camera dry. Cousteau experimented with various options. To make an early underwater film, he used a glass fruit jar and turned the camera on before sealing it inside the jar. He tried using old oil drums with a glass window inserted, sealing all the gaps with rubber to keep water out. Both of these methods worked, but Cousteau needed easier access to the camera to stop and start the film. Eventually, Cousteau enlisted the help of one of his navy contacts, and "Leon Veche, machinist of the torpedo boat *Le Mars*, built a watertight case." It was metal with handles on both sides, so it was easy to carry.

Finding enough light to shoot a movie underwater was also challenging. Cameras—for movies or still photographs—require a lot of light. The shutter on the lens opens to let in enough light to capture the image and then closes again. Under normal conditions, this happens quickly. When the lights are very low, the shutter speed is much slower. It needs that extra time to let in enough light.

When Boutan was taking his underwater photographs, he had almost no light. Even a few feet down, there was a loss of sunlight. At times, he had to leave his shutter open as long as two hours to let enough light in. Therefore, his photos were blurry because everything in front of the lens was in constant motion.

In order to avoid blurry images on film, Cousteau had to find a way to bring down more light. He needed portable lights or a strong flash to brighten the underwater movie set. Once again, Cousteau was going to have to modify existing technology to

This 1892 photograph shows Louis Boutan with his camera. The camera itself is encased in a waterproof box held together by clamps and screws.

suit his dives. Underwater lights existed but he needed them lightweight enough, and equipped with batteries, to carry on the dives. He was already worried that his divers might be carrying too much. Cousteau and his team devised a lightweight battery that could be carried on the diver's belt.

Boutan's blurry undersea picture taken in 1892 demonstrates how difficult it was to capture a clear image underwater.

Trying to make movies during the war provided a unique set of challenges. "We could obtain no 35 mm movie film in wartime," Cousteau said. Instead, he and Simone sat up all night assembling film meant for a still camera. "We bought up fifty-foot rolls of Leica film and spliced the negatives together in a darkroom."

In 1942, Cousteau made a film of Dumas spear fishing. The camera captured him swooping down to spear a fish and returning to the surface. It was just as magnificent to watch on film as it was in real life. Because they were still working on a breathing system, *Ten **Fathoms** Down* was made with the camera operators and actor holding their breath during filming.

Developing a New Breathing Device

Even before Cousteau started, many people had worked on similar underwater breathing devices. Yves Le Prieur was experimenting with his own breathing apparatus in the mid-1920s and an improved version in 1933. A diver wore an air tank of compressed air with a hose attached to a full-face mask. The diver controlled the airflow with his hand so that he could swim freely underwater for ten to twenty minutes—but it was still not ideal.

Yves Le Prieur's system was a definite improvement over previous methods. A diver could roam without a hose attached to a pump, but the airflow was still a problem. It could be switched on and off by hand so the diver could control the flow. When he needed air, he opened the valve then closed it when the mask was full. Unfortunately, it was not precise. A lot of air was wasted, and it was not long before the tank ran out.

It was Cousteau who answered this final dilemma. He used a tank with compressed air, which allowed the diver to carry a greater volume of air in a smaller tank. He also conceived of a release valve for a mouthpiece that would properly regulate his breathing underwater.

When the mouthpiece was held between his teeth and he pressed his tongue against the valve to inhale, or breath in, air was released from the tank. When he exhaled—moving his tongue from the valve—the air stopped flowing from the tank. Because Cousteau was only wearing a mask over his eyes and nose, his exhaled air could easily escape, forming bubbles in the surrounding water. This fact may seem like a small detail, but it was very important.

This c. 1920 photograph shows Yves Le Prieur and his breathing apparatus. A thick stream of air bubbles escapes into the water past his head as the tank rapidly loses air.

Air bubbles escape slowly—at the same pace of a diver's breathing—when a mouthpiece regulator is used.

When we exhale on land, we breathe out a perfectly harmless and natural gas called nitrogen, which then mixes with the air around us. Underwater, however, nitrogen can be dangerous if breathed back in. In an early version of a full-face diving mask, the diver would breath out the nitrogen into his mask, and breathe it back in. Cousteau's release valve, or regulator, allowed a diver to wear a mask that only covered the eyes and nose. By using a regulator that fit in the diver's mouth, he could easily exhale air through his mouth and into the water around him.

Cousteau did not build the valve himself. Simone's father, as director of Air Liquide, helped his son-in-law. He recommended Emile Gagnon, an engineer in Paris. It was Emile who took Cousteau's design and built the valve.

Emile was already working on something similar. He was trying to develop a valve to better control the airflow into a tire. So, he understood immediately what Cousteau wanted. They had to try a few versions before they found the right one. They called their invention the "aqualung," and Jacques could not wait for the moment when he could take it into the water.

Compressed Air

By using pressure, the amount of space that the compressed air takes up in a container—its volume—is decreased. Therefore, a small container can hold a fair amount of air. When air under pressure is released, it can produce a small reaction like giving off a short burst of air. (Think of the sound a can of soda makes when it is opened.) It can also produce a larger reaction like a force powerful enough to stop a train. (Consider the sound a train makes when it stops; that is the air being released by the brakes, which stops the wheels.) Compressed air is used in some heavy machines, train brakes, tires, and air tanks for deep-sea divers. Larger volumes of air can fit into small tanks making it possible for a diver to carry their own tank on their back.

The tank carried by a diver contains enough compressed air for the swimmer to breath underwater for a long time. The hose with the mouthpiece regulator is attached to the tank.

CHAPTER 4

Beneath the Waves

*No children ever opened a Christmas present with
more excitement than ours when we unpacked the
first "aqualung." If it worked, diving could
be revolutionized.*

When the first aqualung finally arrived from Paris,
Cousteau could barely contain his excitement. "No
children ever opened a Christmas present with more
excitement," he later wrote. Cousteau took his prized
possession and rushed to the seaside. He wanted to try it
out right away.

On a warm June day
in 1943, Jacques-Yves
Cousteau stood on the
shore of the Mediterranean.
He had three cylinders of
compressed air strapped to
his back. He was wearing a
dark bathing suit, flippers
on his feet, and a diving
mask. Jacques, a tall, very

Cousteau first tested his aqualung
in 1943. Since then it has become
the principal piece of equipment
for underwater exploration. This
1956 photograph shows Jacques
Cousteau in a very familiar pose:
standing on the deck of a ship with
an air tank on his back.

thin man, was quite a sight. He looked even more peculiar as he waddled toward the water, staggering slightly under the weight of the equipment. Cousteau was anxious to submerge and test his new underwater invention, but he stood there, trying to savor every moment. He had worked so hard for this day.

Cousteau put the regulator to his mouth, gripping the valve between his teeth. He nodded to his wife Simone, Frederic Dumas, and Philippe Tailliez, and then Cousteau moved slowly into the sea.

The swimmer kicked his feet, gliding smoothly down into the water. He pressed his tongue against the valve and took one deep breath—his lungs filled with air—then exhaled. His breath escaped around his mouthpiece in a stream of bubbles. Cousteau took another deep breath and exhaled. The aqualung worked! He was breathing underwater and controlling his air supply perfectly. Jacques kicked his feet and fanned his arms toward his side, propelling himself into deeper depths.

Simone swam along the surface of the water with a mask and snorkel. She kept watch on her husband below. If she saw any sign of trouble, she would notify Frederic Dumas. Frederic was prepared to dive deep—he could hold his breath and go as deep as sixty feet—to rescue his friend. Thankfully, though, all was well. Cousteau looked up to the surface. "In the center of the looking glass was the trim silhouette of Simone, reduced to a doll. I waved. The doll waved at me."

The aqualung worked! He was breathing underwater and controlling his air supply perfectly.

Cousteau swam along the ocean floor, among the fish and reeds and rocks, diving as deep as sixty feet. He could follow the fish, stop to overturn rocks, and explore caves without worrying about his air supply. He had a perfect view of the world around him thanks to his diving mask. He could at last take the time to touch and examine everything he saw because of the aqualung.

Floating in the Silent World

It was peaceful and quiet, and he felt perfectly relaxed. "I experimented with all possible maneuvers of the aqualung—loops, somersaults and barrel rolls," Cousteau said. Even skin divers, those who went down without any equipment with the possible exception of goggles or masks, did not have as much freedom—playfully swimming and spinning would take up too much energy. They only had a small amount of time before having to go back up for air. With the aqualung, Cousteau could stay underwater for what seemed like a lifetime—then when he surfaced, he felt like only a few minutes had passed, even though he had been below for over thirty.

Cousteau never lost the excitement and fascination he experienced on that first time with the aqualung. "Diving is the most fabulous satisfaction you can experience," Cousteau said in an interview many years later. "I am miserable out of water."

In his book *The Silent World*, Jacques wrote that he used to dream about flying. He would wake up with dreamlike memories of soaring over trees and water. However, everything changed after that day in 1943. He was no longer a man interested in conquering the skies. "Since that first aqualung flight, I have never had a dream of flying," he said.

Although World War II was still raging, that summer was a magical time for them all. Jacques, Simone, and their sons were living in a house called Villa Barry. Philippe Tailliez and his family, their camera operator, Claude Houlbreque, and Frederic Dumas all lived with them. As Cousteau said, "To the occupying troops we must have seemed a wistful holiday party."

During the summer months of 1943, Jacques and his friends went on as many as 500 dives. Dumas dived to a depth of 210 feet. To go so deep without a submarine or diving bell was an incredible feat. Until Dumas made his successful dive, no one knew if the human body could survive that level of pressure. They improved on their designs after these trials. They fixed the weight of the tanks so they weren't too heavy. They modified their masks so they fit more comfortably. They searched for comfortable suits for cold-water dives. Simply put, they did everything they could to improve and perfect the aqualung and their diving experience.

Cousteau never lost the excitement and fascination he experienced on that first time with the aqualung.

An Underwater Movie Studio

With all of the aqualung testing, Cousteau had not forgotten about his underwater movies. He had the "perfect movie studio"

Sunken ships, such as the one shown in this 1993 photo taken near St. Croix, became the perfect subject for Cousteau's film *Wrecks*.

Sunken Treasure

When a ship goes down, it continues to sink farther and farther into the ocean floor, and a great deal of digging may be required in order to salvage anything from that ship. Typically, people imagine sunken treasure ships filled with pirate's gold and silver. The truth is, that is not the kind of treasure most ships offer. There is usually very little gold to be found—pirate's gold or otherwise—but these ships often provide their own source of treasure. For example, modern sunken ships may carry tons of valuable metals, such as tin, copper, and wolfram that are waiting to be found.

Cousteau tells the story of an amateur treasure hunter on the Riviera. One day, the man was salvaging an old wreck. When Cousteau asked if he found anything valuable, the treasure hunter proudly said, "Cocoa beans!" Apparently, the man dragged the beans onto shore and dried them in the sun. When he sold the beans to a wholesaler, he received $25,000. As Cousteau wrote, "This proves that there really is treasure under the sea."

Some sunken treasures can survive many years with little damage. In this 1977 photograph, a diver uncovers a pot that is more than 1,000 old near the coast of Turkey.

in mind for their film projects. Sunken ships! There were many ships on the ocean floor—some had been underwater for hundreds (some for thousands) of years—but the challenge was finding them. The aqualung would now make it easier. Divers could roam freely looking for a ship and exploring its battered deck.

The result was a short film called *Wrecks*. Cousteau and his team took it to Cannes, a city on the Riviera that was hosting a new film festival. *Wrecks* won a prize for "best short" in May 1943.

France Is Liberated

In 1944, France was liberated by American, British, and Canadian forces. The Second World War would continue for another year but the French people were at long last free from German and Italian rule. However, not everyone was opposed to the German occupation. There were men and women in France who supported German rule in France and actively collaborated to keep them in power. Pierre Cousteau, Jacques's older brother fell into this camp.

A photograph captures the celebration in the streets as Allied troops drive through a newly liberated Paris on August 25, 1944.

Nevertheless, the French Government was very impressed with Captain Jacques Cousteau's work during the war. They awarded him medals for his bravery in the French Resistance and for his work with the aqualung. He had revolutionized diving and changed the way that the world viewed the ocean. When Cousteau suggested that he head a new research group to study the ocean, the French navy happily agreed. It would be the start of a very productive working relationship.

Pierre Cousteau (1906–1959)

Pierre Cousteau, Jacques's older brother, was a newspaper writer and editor who wrote pro-**fascist** and **Nazi** articles in the 1930s. Although he was sentenced to a life in prison at the end of the war because of his support of the Germans and Nazi Party, he was released only a few years later. Pierre lived in Paris with his second wife and children, but he and Jacques were never close again. Pierre Cousteau published books about his life as a collaborator, attempts to flee the country after the war, and his time in prison. He passed away in 1959 from cancer.

After the liberation, Pierre Cousteau, like the collaborators shown in this 1944 photograph, were arrested and tried.

CHAPTER 5

Unexpected Dangers

Our worst experience in five thousand dives did not come in the sea but in an inland water cave, the famous Fontaine-de-Vaucluse near Avignon.

By the fall of 1945, World War II was over, and Captain Jacques Cousteau was set to return to regular naval duties. He was assigned to a port in Marseilles but felt other work was better suited to him. "My job was useful but it seemed to me that any officer could do it," Cousteau said. He knew he could contribute more as a diver.

Cousteau traveled to Paris to show *Wrecks* to Admiral Andre G. Lemonnier. Cousteau described the advantages of using the aqualung for naval work. The admiral was duly impressed. Cousteau returned to Toulon with orders to start a new diving office—the Undersea Research Group. Philippe Tailliez was assigned to the office, and Frederic Dumas joined as a civilian employee.

Cousteau and his team outfitted the *Elie Monnier*, their navy-assigned boat, to their needs. They added a diving platform and decompression chamber in case a diver surfaced with the bends. The navy allowed Cousteau time to explore on his own, but there was still important work to be done.

"Mine recovery was not one of the paramount aims of the Undersea Research Group," Cousteau said, but life on the Mediterranean was still dangerous. The sea surrounding Toulon was populated by mines left by the

This 1947 photograph shows the crew of the Underwater Research Group aboard the *Elie Monnier*. Cousteau stands on the far left.

German navy. While contact mines were still hidden below the water's surface, the French navy could not clear the area or salvage ships, and fishing boats had difficulty navigating the waters.

Cousteau's job was to locate mines then notify the demolition experts who defused them. His group used their skills as divers and underwater filmmakers to record their findings. Even though they were doing something that they loved, they all knew the danger involved in their work. Mines could be detonated by touch or sound waves through the water, and they had to be extraordinarily careful. It was a slow, sometimes painful job, but Cousteau and his crew did not waiver.

Whenever a new crewmember joined the team, the diver was trained to use the aqualung. It was not long before Cousteau had a ship full of brave men, all ready to dive, explore, and risk their lives.

Naval Mines or Floating Contact Mines

Naval mines were explosive devices—bombs—left in the water. They were designed to explode primarily upon contact with a ship. They have been in use for hundreds of years—in China in the 1300s and in the American Civil War—and can still be found today. Because they are submerged in the water, they are not easy to detect and are therefore an effective wartime weapon.

The mines that Cousteau and crew encountered were large round steel balls with metal spikes or rods sticking out. The mines were attached to the ocean floor by a cable to prevent them from floating away. These mines might weigh as much as five hundred pounds, and their explosion could sink a battleship.

This image shows the metal rods sticking out of a round mine. Any pressure on these spikes could cause the mine to explode.

Teaching His Sons

In the summer of 1945, Cousteau decided it was time to show his young sons the undersea world, and to teach them the joy of diving. With mini-aqualungs designed especially for them, Jacques led Jean-Michel, aged seven, and Philippe, aged five, into the sea. Jacques recounted their happy responses. "The peaceful water resounded with screams of delight as they pointed out all the wonders to me."

In the summer of 1945, Cousteau decided it was time to show his young sons the undersea world . . .

Throughout that summer, Jean-Michel and Philippe joined their father in the water, and they were soon expert divers. Simone came along with them or watched them carefully from shore or over the side of a boat. When Jacques's schedule allowed, the family enjoyed seaside picnics as "Jean-Michel would go down thirty feet with a kitchen fork and fetch succulent sea urchins."

When fall arrived, the boys were sent away to school. Cousteau was working all the time, and Simone was always at his side. The boys returned for holidays and summers, and the family continued to dive whenever they could.

Exploring the Fontaine-de-Vaucluse

Through all of Cousteau's years exploring, and his time inventing the aqualung, he faced danger whenever he took to the sea, but he never took unnecessary risks. "We have always placed a reasonable premium on returning alive," Cousteau said. "Even Didi, the boldest among us, is not a stunt man." So, it came as a great surprise to them all, when the team almost met with a bitter end in August 1946.

"Our worst experience in five thousand dives did not come in the sea," as Cousteau describes it, "but in an inland water cave, the famous Fontaine-de-Vaucluse near Avignon."

For most of the year, the fountain is a calm pool tucked into the limestone cliffs of a mountain. It is actually the mouth of a cave that extends below the surface of the water. An underground river flows through the cave and no one knows its depth. In late winter or early spring, this quiet pool erupts into a seventy-five-foot fountain of water that suddenly gushes into the sky and creates a tremendous waterfall along the limestone.

No one in Cousteau's team was certain why this happened or why with such force. It was suspected that a nearby river was the source of the pool water, but no one had traced the path of

The mouth of the cave at the Fontaine-de-Vaucluse is pictured in an undated photograph. Although the water appears calm, it erupts into a seventy-five foot fountain during late winter.

the underwater cave. Cousteau decided that he and his men would find out.

They were not the first to investigate the cave below the fountain. A man named Senor Negri attempted the journey in 1936. According to Negri's account, he descended 120 feet into the cave, but stopped because his air hose was caught on a rock, and he could go no farther.

Cousteau and Dumas tried to talk to Negri to confirm this information, but he refused to see them. There was no written evidence of Negri's dive, only stories. For his descent, Negri put a microphone in his helmet to transmit the details as they were happening. So, Cousteau and his team planned their dive based on the stories of townsfolk who were listening on shore to Negri's transmission. Unfortunately, Jacques did not realize until it was too late that Negri exaggerated his descent into the cave.

Even though they had been using the aqualung for three years and several thousand dives, Cousteau was still perfecting the apparatus. They decided to test revisions and redesigns on their equipment by using it on the cave dives. To compensate for this risk, they prepared well for each dive by researching the cave as best they could.

It was decided that Cousteau and Dumas would descend first. They both wore diving suits with woolen undergarments for extra warmth. Even though it was August, the waters of the cave would likely be very cold. They had flashlights, rope, and an ice pick to help them climb. The two men attached themselves together with rope as they did not want to lose each other in the dark. Simone, worried about the new

They tried to think of every emergency so that they would not be caught short.

Cousteau, seen in this undated photograph in full diving gear, was careful when preparing for a dive. He always wanted to be ready for any emergency that might occur.

equipment and an unknown cave, could not wait on shore as usual. Instead, she went to the town to sit in a café.

They tried to think of every emergency so they would not be caught short. The rope was their only means of communication with the surface crew waiting in a canoe. If there were an emergency, one of the divers would signal the crew by pulling on the rope.

A Rope Too Long

Cousteau and Dumas met trouble right away. In order to descend into the cave, the divers had to travel through a narrow tunnel, also known as a shaft. The shaft was not as Negri described it. He claimed it would be on an angle but instead it went almost straight down. Before they had a chance to take hold of the walls, they dropped quickly down, crashing into walls and rocks along the way. Dumas's suit filled with water and Jacques lost the extra rope he was carrying. They landed in a cave that sat at least 150 feet—much lower than Negri described—below the surface. This cave was nothing like Negri described. There was no uphill slope as claimed. There was one other shaft and it led down. They were already in a difficult situation, so they would have to return the way they came. Cousteau assessed their situation. He knew they would have to act quickly.

Dumas was in trouble. He was having difficulty breathing in compressed air and he was beginning to lose consciousness. They both started to feel terribly drowsy and heavy limbed. Cousteau thought this must be due to the sudden drop in pressure. He noticed his friend struggling as he floated against the cave ceiling. Although he was confused and his ears hurt, Cousteau summoned all his strength to get them to the surface.

Cousteau and Dumas met trouble right away.

Pulling Dumas with him, Jacques took hold of the guide rope. He was feeling confused and lightheaded. He was so focused on reaching the surface with Dumas that he forgot all their prearranged signals. As he started to climb, he tugged on the rope three times as one hand reached over the other. His crew misunderstood this motion. Three tugs was their signal for more rope. His crew did just as he asked—they let out more rope into the cave below.

At first, as the rope started to slacken, Jacques almost panicked. Why were they letting out more rope? His crew was doing their job perfectly, but was in fact doing more harm then good. Cousteau tried to concentrate on what he should do next.

He decided to let them continue handing down rope. He knew they would never let go when they reached the end. The rope would tighten when there was no more to give and then he could climb up. Jacques waited until 400 feet of rope lay at his feet.

. . . Cousteau summoned all his strength to get them to the surface.

The rope did not tighten, though. Instead, Jacques felt a knot in his hand. His team had tied two ropes together! They had such faith that the dive was going well that they were giving them more rope. Jacques had no choice. He was going to have to climb out while pulling the weakened Dumas behind him.

Jacques very slowly made his way up the rock wall of the shaft. It was slow, painful work, especially when he was already so confused and drowsy. In all of his dives, he had never experienced this sensation before. Cousteau made it only a few dozen feet up the rock before the weight of Dumas pulled him back down.

They were in serious trouble. Jacques was starting to worry that they would not make it out alive. Dumas was unable to help, and Cousteau doubted he had the strength to drag them both to the surface. He held on to the rope, bracing against the rock for support and clutching Dumas's limp body. Cousteau knew there was something else—something that his foggy and confused brain had forgotten.

Back from the Jaws of Death

Suddenly, it came to him—their distress signal! He gave the rope six tugs, hoping that his message would be received.

By this time, Jacques was so weak that his crew could barely feel the tugs. The rope shook only slightly, but they decided not to take a chance and started to pull the rope back up. Jacques hung on while he and Dumas were raised to the surface. Both men were sick and weak and very happy to breathe fresh air again.

Of course, they were not as happy as Simone. The men were already calmly discussing their dive on shore when she rushed to hug and kiss them. The villagers had told her that one of the divers had drowned in the caves. She raced from the café in wild panic to find the men recovering on shore. For Simone, it was almost as if her husband and Dumas had risen from the dead.

Later that day, other members of the team, including Philippe Tailliez, tried the dive. They hoped that knowing the correct information about the shaft would help. They had the same reaction, though. They felt drugged and listless. Once again, the divers made it back to the surface just in time. After careful examination of their air tanks, they realized there was a leak. They were breathing in poisoned air rather than compressed air all the time they were underwater. It was a good reminder to check and recheck equipment before each dive. It also emphasized the importance of having a good team with you at all times.

Once again, the divers made it back to the surface just in time.

The Fontaine-de-Vaucluse

Senor Negri was not the first to explore the cave. He followed in the footsteps of Ottonelli, a diver from Marseilles. Ottonelli descended into the cave in a diving suit in 1878. He reached a depth of ninety feet—dropping a zinc weight another thirty feet to test depth—before returning to the surface. His zinc weight was not recovered even though Negri claims he saw it during his descent.

Today, the fountain and the surrounding town are popular tourist attractions. People come to enjoy the tranquil pond or to admire the tremendous fountain when it is active. No diver has explored the underground river below the fountain so no one knows exactly how far or how deep it goes. However, a robot submarine with a camera reached a depth of 1,000 feet in 1985.

The river of the Fontaine-de-Vaucluse flows through the center of town. The water is peaceful and quiet until the fountain erupts once a year.

CHAPTER 6

The *Calypso*

We must go and see for ourselves.

By 1950, the Undersea Research Group had a building of its own. It contained a laboratory, a workshop for building new equipment, a film lab, and quarters for the crew. Cousteau's work with the navy was very important, but he was spending more and more time exploring and filming. He wanted to look beyond the areas the navy assigned him. He wanted the freedom to search new regions and discover new shipwrecks. If he was going to accomplish all he wanted, he was going to need something more than ambition. He was going to need his own ship.

Through Simone's family connections, Cousteau met Sir Loel Guinness, an Irish politician. Guinness was fascinated by Cousteau's stories of diving and shipwrecks. When Cousteau explained his plans to not only explore and discover but also to share all his findings, Guinness promised to secure a ship for Jacques.

Calypso's Past

It was the *Calypso*. She—ships are traditionally referred to as female—arrived in Toulon in July 1950. Guinness did not give the ship to Cousteau. Instead, Guinness set up a fund to pay for the ship and her repairs. They made an agreement that Cousteau would pay him a token of one franc (a French dollar) a year.

The *Calypso* was 140 feet long and 24 feet across. She had twin engines and a wooden hull. Built in the United States, she went to work as a minesweeper for the British navy during World War II. After the war, she was sold to a private company and used as a ferry in Crete. It was there that she was given the name *Calypso*, a sea nymph, or beautiful woman, from Greek mythology.

Cousteau and his team had extensive plans for the *Calypso*. They intended to refit her to all their needs. She would soon be the perfect research vessel for them. There was a lot of work ahead. Cousteau knew there would be little time for naval work. The navy administration agreed to give Cousteau a three-year leave of absence. Even though it was originally founded with assistance from the navy, the Undersea Research Group stayed under Cousteau's command.

The *Calypso*, would appear in all of Cousteau's films. In this 1983 photograph, the *Calypso* arrives in St. Louis, Missouri, to film a documentary about the Mississippi River.

Outfitting the *Calypso*

Even though the *Calypso* came to them almost free of charge, they still needed a lot of money to pay for all of her alterations. This was not a navy project so it would not provide the funds, and Jacques and Simone did not have much money of their own. Simone was from a wealthy family, but they were living on his navy salary. In order to pay for fuel, a new compass, and other instruments for the *Calypso*, Simone sold her furs and some family jewels. Perhaps she suspected she would have little use for a fur coat when her normal attire was an aqualung.

Jacques and Simone made the common area and living quarters of the *Calypso* as comfortable as possible. The team worked closely together and spent a lot of time in a small space. It was important that everyone got along. They had to rely on each other even in dangerous situations. They would have to face long dives, the bends, exhaustion, injuries, possible shark attacks, storms at sea, and equipment failure. Cousteau made certain that comfort and rest would not be an added concern for his crew. The *Calypso* was not a luxurious or fancy ship, but she was home.

The Calypso *was not a luxurious or fancy ship, but she was home.*

A decompression chamber was installed on deck and a diving platform on the back of the ship. An observation tower was built at the front of the ship that doubled as a radio antenna and **crow's nest**. Also at the front of the ship, just below sea level, Cousteau built one of *Calypso*'s most interesting features: a "false nose."

The false nose was an observation deck a few feet below the surface of the water. "The bulbous chamber had eight portholes that enabled a few of *Calypso's* crew to see and film underwater without even leaving the ship." Crewmembers could look through these portholes and watch the abundance of ocean life undisturbed. It was a nice, peaceful place to sit and think.

The first trip aboard the redesigned *Calypso* took place in June 1951. Cousteau, Simone, Dumas, and a few friends took the *Calypso* out for a short run through the Mediterranean to test the new equipment. It was a momentous occasion and all on board felt the excitement. Before they left port, though, Jacques made one more addition. He hung up a sign that read—*Il faut aller voir*—"We must go and see for ourselves." This was Cousteau's personal philosophy and the *Calypso's* motto.

Cousteau had a "false nose" built into the front of the *Calypso* for observation purposes. It was much smaller than the observation window that was featured on the *Nautilus,* as seen in this illustration from an 1870 edition of *20,000 Leagues Under the Sea,* but served the same purpose.

Although the French navy often assisted Cousteau in his ventures, it no longer offered financial support. Knowing that any future excursions and explorations pursued by the Undersea Research Group would require financing, Cousteau set up a nonprofit organization. The French Oceanographic Expeditions, also known as the COF (its French name was *Campagnes Océanographiques Françaises*), would fund all of *Calypso*'s journeys. The COF would raise the money "from fees from *Calypso*'s privately sponsored research, from grants, and from royalties on films, books, articles, and television specials."

Calypso's First Expedition

On November 24, 1951, the *Calypso* set sail for the Red Sea. It was heading toward the Farasan archipelago, a chain of islands near the coast of Saudi Arabia. This was one of the world's most complex coral reefs. It was so complex, in fact, that no one had

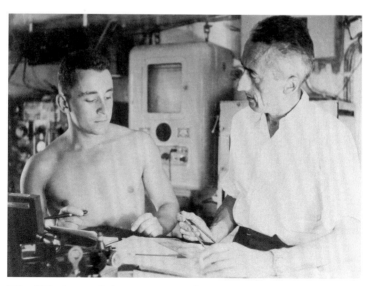

This c. 1960 photograph shows Cousteau on the *Calypso* looking over charts and maps with a crewmember.

mapped the entire chain. Cousteau and his *Calypso* crew would try to do so.

Cousteau loved diving near coral reefs. They were one of the first things he encountered when he ventured into the Mediterranean. Cousteau considered these reefs as one of the greatest symbols of life and beauty under the sea. Although Cousteau would one day be a wonderful advocate for preserving reefs, there was a time when he was guilty of destructive practices. In his earlier books and films, he talks about dynamiting and breaking away coral to search for ships and treasures. This is something he regretted in later years.

Although Cousteau loved the beauty of the reef, he was less in awe of this natural wonder when he was on board a ship. Piloting a boat over or around coral reefs is potentially dangerous. A reef can snag a ship's bottom and rip a hole in hit, causing the boat to sink. Wherever waters are populated by coral reefs, there is usually a graveyard of sunken ships.

Cousteau and his team quickly learned how to read the sea around them. From the bridge or crow's nest, they carefully examined the color of the water. "Brown or white was danger—a reef near the surface. There was a wide range of subtle greens from which to interpret depth, and dark blue was easy sailing."

Cousteau and his team quickly learned how to read the sea around them.

Of course, the *Calypso* crew did not only rely on personal observation to examine the waters around them. The ship was equipped with state-of-the-art equipment, including a sonar system. By sending sound waves into the water, they could map out the ocean floor and coral patterns beneath them. This sonar system also proved valuable when locating buried minerals, such as oil, by determining the depth of the soil or rock bed.

Coral Reefs

Coral reefs are sometimes called the Gardens of the Sea. Although they may look like an old skeleton or shell, they are actually living organisms. They breathe and grow like any other sea creature. As Cousteau described, "Each square foot was a **microcosm** of worms, tiny hairy crabs, flowering slugs, and carousing vermin."

Most reefs are found in shallow tropical waters. There was a time, not so long ago, when these coral reefs were found throughout the southern hemisphere. Today, due to pollution, over fishing, and disrespectful divers breaking off pieces as souvenirs, a great deal of them have been destroyed or are disappearing.

This photograph shows the variety of color, plant, and marine life that can be found on or near a coral reef.

The *Calypso* returned to Toulon on February 5, 1952. Their voyage to the Red Sea was a success. They had mapped the coral reef, made hundreds of dives, and filmed loads of marine life. With the aid of divers, the team of scientists on board gathered numerous samples of **flora and fauna**, some of them previously unknown species. The *Calypso* was well equipped with scientific labs to conduct research, and had ample storage space for holding specimens to bring back to museums and universities.

An Archeological Expedition

After a very short rest and some ship repairs, the *Calypso* and crew were back at sea, sailing for Marseilles, France, in July 1952. Cousteau heard a story from a lobster fisherman about an old sunken ship near the coast. They decided to investigate.

Dumas made the first dive and saw nothing. There was no sign of a ship anywhere in the vicinity. Even though Cousteau trusted Dumas's observational skills, he went below for a look. He was just about to resurface when he noticed some dishes and jars. He brought two goblets up for the archeologist from a Marseilles museum to examine. Professor Benoît declared they were from the third century BCE—during the Roman Empire.

Cousteau understood immediately the importance of this find. He and the crew got to work right away. They established a camp at Grand Congloué, which they christened "Port Calypso." The sunken ship was not far off shore, but it sat more than one hundred feet underwater. Knowing this would be a long underwater **excavation**, they set up huts where a few men could spend the winter while working. The *Calypso* would travel back and forth from Marseilles, depending on the weather.

The men made dozens of dives each day. They had to break through coral, rock, and silt to unearth the treasures. There was

Sonar Systems

With a sonar system, sound waves are sent from a ship through the water below. When these waves hit an object (a submarine, a sunken ship, a school of fish, etc.), they bounce back up to the ship. A sonar system reads these echoes and creates a map. This is how objects are located underwater and how maps of the ocean floor are made. Sonar systems are found in the natural world, too. Bats and dolphins use sound waves to find their way. In nature, this is called echolocation.

Sound waves from a sonar system can produce images, such as the one shown here, taken in 1983 of the USS *Meredith*, which sank in 1944 near the coast of Normandy.

too much debris for the men to carry so they used a system called an airlift to clear the way. The airlift was a hose 150 feet long attached to a pump on shore. The divers guided the hose over the area and the hose sucked up the silt. They had to be careful while they worked with this powerful hose. They did not discover until it was too late that they were also picking up some of the treasure, accidentally smashing 2,000-year-old plates.

This photograph from the 1990s shows a diver using a vacuum to dig a hole over a shipwreck. This apparatus is very similar to the one that Cousteau used at Grand Congloué.

By July 1953, Cousteau and crew had collected more than 10,000 artifacts, conducted 3,500 dives, and dived as deep as 140 feet. Cousteau considered this more than a hunt for treasure. A sunken ship "contains history. It tells us about men who lived and suffered in a land that was, at that time, at the very edge of the world."

To pay tribute to their recovered treasure, the men gathered for dinner at Port Calypso. They wore togas—as men did in ancient Rome—and ate from the dishes they rescued from the sea. During the celebration, the men lifted goblets in salute to their team and the Roman sailors who brought them there.

A sunken ship "contains history. It tells us about men who lived and suffered in a land that was, at that time, at the very edge of the world."

On September 22, 1952, Albert Falco joined the team as a diver. Falco would stay with the *Calypso* team for almost forty years and eventually serve as chief diver. Along with Frederic Dumseries and join him on all the *Calypso* expeditions. In 1952, though, Falco was simply an eager young diver, happy to join this new adventure.

Another Cousteau Office

While on a return trip to Toulon in 1953, Cousteau broadened the scope of the Undersea Research Group. It would now develop and build new equipment as needed. At Port Calypso, his team was forced to find innovative ways to work, creating makeshift equipment on the spot to get the job done. The company would invent and build new equipment so the crew could get their work done without delay.

Cousteau discovered that as they added more equipment and projects became more elaborate, further changes to the *Calypso* were necessary. For instance, when the scientists at Port Calypso—who were not divers—wanted to see the shipwreck, the crew set up equipment on board for remote television cameras and for a monitor so the eager observers could watch from the shore. Cousteau also added a film-developing lab to the *Calypso*.

Albert Falco (left), pictured here with Cousteau in 1953, was a valuable member of Cousteau's team. He would appear in almost all of Cousteau's documentaries.

CHAPTER 7

The Silent World Below

Soon, perhaps, we will all realize that the sea is but an immense extension of our human world, a province of our universe, a patrimony that we must protect if we ourselves are to survive.

In 1953, Jacques Cousteau published a book that he co-wrote with Frederic Dumas. *The Silent World* told the history of the aqualung and Cousteau's early experiences diving in the Mediterranean. They also recalled their adventures while exploring sunken ships, and their near-death experience at the Fontaine-de-Vaucluse.

The book also included Cousteau's 1948 work with Auguste Piccard, who had invited Cousteau to join him on a deep-sea dive in his submersible vehicle called a "bathyscaphe." Piccard had devoted many years of his life to this project and he wanted Cousteau to join him.

Cousteau's family saw this mission as some kind of "craziness"—probably because the bathyscaphe went to depths thousands of feet under water—and they tried to talk him out of it. They had little to worry about, though.

The paperback cover of *The Silent World* is pictured here. The book was the first of many that Cousteau wrote about exploring the sea. He authored, coauthored, and edited dozens of books.

Diving Submersibles

Diving submersibles are vessels made for deep-diving exploration. The bathyscaphe, invented by Auguste Piccard, is a type of diving submersible that can be propelled in extremely deep waters. The bathysphere, is a spherical diving submersible that is lowered into the water by very long cables. William Beebe, an American explorer and scientist, used a bathysphere to dive 3,028 feet in 1934. He made a live radio broadcast during his dive so all of America could travel with him. He reported, among other things, seeing fantastical creatures such as fish that glowed in the dark. At the time, this was thought to be an illusion of Beebe's. Only years later were these fish viewed by others.

In 1960, the *Trieste*, a bathyscaphe, dropped to a remarkable 35,800 feet in the Mariana Trench, the deepest part of any ocean. At the time, this was the deepest dive on record, and the *Trieste* was piloted by Jacques Piccard, Auguste's son.

William Beebe (left) and Otis Barton, an engineer who worked with him, stand beside their bathysphere in a 1934 photograph.

Cousteau was not on board when Piccard's bathyscaphe made its deepest dive to 4,600 feet and was too badly damaged for another trip down.

Five million copies of *The Silent World* were sold, and it was translated into twenty-two languages. As one reviewer said, "Jacques-Yves Cousteau, inventor of the aqualung, describes his underwater adventures with a scientist's care and a poet's feeling."

A 1948 photograph shows Jacques Piccard making final preparations to take the bathyscaphe into the deep. His son Auguste stands at his side while last-minute plans are made.

Seeing True Colors

Cousteau was pleased and slightly amazed by how fascinated people were with his story. It was inspiring, especially because there was still so much more to share. Cousteau was a firm believer that seeing was believing.

In 1953, the same year that his book came out, Cousteau asked an expert in the field of underwater photography to join the crew. Dr. Harold Edgerton of the Massachusetts Institute of

Technology "has been the most imaginative and obstinate mind in turning deep-sea photography into a practical, indispensable tool." He and Cousteau were committed to discovering a better flash-and-lighting system for underwater filmmaking and deep-sea photography.

One of the things that Cousteau wanted to capture and show was the wonderful array of colors below, but filming under water presented its own set of problems. For one thing, light passing through water affects how the color is captured on film. He wanted to show the true colors of certain plants and animals as they appeared in their natural habitat. He could bring a blue fish to the surface but it would not keep the same color it did when swimming on the ocean floor. Bright multicolored coral seemed to fade when it reached the air. Capturing these true colors was Cousteau's goal.

This color photograph shows Cousteau underwater, holding a small movie camera. His team—with Edgerton—worked hard to invent easy-to-carry underwater cameras that captured the wonders of the deep.

Another problem Cousteau encountered with underwater filming was that the colors Cousteau saw below the water were not the colors appearing on film. "At fifteen feet red turned pink, and at forty feet became virtual black." Edgerton's flash system solved this problem. The colors captured on film were as close to real life as they could hope.

Oil Company Contracts

Cousteau and the *Calypso* left for the Persian Gulf in January 1954 to fulfill a contract with a British oil company to survey the ocean for buried mineral deposits. Contracts like this helped Cousteau in two ways. First of all, it provided funds for expeditions. Second, it was another opportunity for Cousteau and his men to explore new areas. The oil companies were looking for new reserves so it was an excuse for the *Calypso* to visit out-of-the-way places.

Even though Cousteau returned to the French Riviera at the end of every venture, he and Simone did not stay in one place for long. Cousteau was always working on the next expedition or the one after that, flying to meet new contacts for work and funding, writing a book, planning a film, or designing new equipment. Simone often traveled with her husband or stayed on the *Calypso* with the crew. The Undersea Research Group was always working several steps ahead, constructing new equipment and preparing for their next adventure. By 1955, they were building the first prototype of the diving saucer, a two-man mini submarine.

Filming *The Silent World*

With the successful advancements in underwater filming, Cousteau set about to capture on film almost all of the adventures chronicled in his book, *The Silent World*. Cousteau recruited a young filmmaker named Louis Malle as the camera operator. Malle lived, worked, and dived with the crew for months, filming everything as it happened.

The film *The Silent World*—released in 1956—showed life on the *Calypso* for the crew. The cameras caught them eating their meals and relaxing with one another. The cameras followed as they traveled the Mediterranean. They were filmed during dive after dive as they swam along decks of sunken ships and passed by the bright colors of coral reefs. At one location, a grouper fish—nicknamed Ulysses by the crew—had a guest-starring role. At first, the crew was charmed by the fish as it swam alongside them and played. Eventually, though, it disturbed scenes, bumping equipment and swimming into shots, making a general pest of itself. Finally, they had to trap it in a cage during filming so they could continue working in peace. Later on, though, Cousteau admitted that Ulysses was the star of the movie.

The film version of *The Silent World* also showed less pleasant aspects of life on the *Calypso*. The crew was filmed throwing sticks of dynamite into a bay so they could easily collect sea specimens. Another time, the crew was surprised by a group of whales swimming beside the *Calypso*. It was a lovely moment until a baby whale was caught in

A French movie poster advertises *Le Monde du Silence*, the French title for *The Silent World*. The film received a great deal of attention and made Cousteau a star.

the ship's propeller and was killed. When sharks arrived to eat the whale, the *Calypso* crew became infuriated. "They hauled flipping sharks onto the deck in a production line and finished them off."

The Silent World won the most prestigious prize—the Palme d'Or—at the Cannes Film Festival that year. It also won the

Cousteau and crew haul a sperm whale onto the *Calypso* in a scene from *The Silent World*. For many viewers, these up-close images of marine life provided a completely new experience.

Academy Award for best documentary. (Cousteau would eventually win three Academy Awards in total.) Before *The Silent World* Cousteau had made several short films—including some for the National Geographic Society that aired on television—but *The Silent World* film suddenly put him in a new league.

Jacques Cousteau was becoming an international celebrity. Magazines wanted to interview him, and he started writing articles for *National Geographic* magazine. He appeared on television talk shows in France and Britain. He was even a guest on the American game show *What's My Line?* in which blindfolded contestants had to guess his identity.

Until this time, Cousteau was technically still in the French navy. He was able to go on so many explorations, write books, make movies, and help design new equipment because the navy allowed it. It either gave him leave or assignments that would require little time. Cousteau now realized he could be of more service to humanity by exploring and educating than by fulfilling naval duties. It was time to resign his post and consider his next step.

Cousteau (third from right) and a group of French actors stand on the deck of the *Calypso* during the 1956 Cannes Film Festival. Cousteau was celebrating his win for best film at the festival.

A New Challenge

Thankfully, the perfect opportunity soon presented itself. Cousteau was offered and accepted the position of Director for the Oceanographic Institute in Monaco. The once-thriving institute had fallen on hard times, and Monaco's monarch Prince Rainier wanted to restore it to its former glory. Cousteau's knack for publicity would be a great help as would his curiosity for the undiscovered underwater world. Cousteau was, once again, starting a new and exciting adventure.

Some people were surprised by Cousteau's appointment to the Oceanographic Institute. He had no formal training as a scientist, technician, or educator. He had no experience running an organization that large or with so many responsibilities.

Cousteau was, once again, starting a new and exciting adventure.

However, he did have confidence. He immediately got to work promoting the institute and raising funds. His work as an explorer benefited his work as director. Whenever people heard about his adventures, they also learned about the institute. It was not long before the Oceanographic Institute of Monaco was once again a busy and bustling environment.

Cousteau had big plans for the institute and the projects—including his own—that it would fund. He ordered a new aquarium and brought in dolphins and other specimens to attract tourists. He ordered or built new equipment and renovated the labs, storage spaces, and display areas. The institute's board of directors was alarmed by all this spending and tried to put a stop to it. However, Prince Rainier stepped in and approved the expenses, even encouraging Cousteau to build and explore to his heart's content. The prince was a great supporter of Cousteau's and continued to be for many years. Cousteau held the position of director at the Institute until 1988.

Monaco's Oceanographic Institute

Prince Albert I of Monaco started the institute in 1910, the same year that Cousteau was born. The stately building overlooking the Mediterranean housed aquariums, a large resource library, and a collection of plants and animals for study. The prince had a great interest in science and research. He also founded an archeology museum in Paris and funded many explorations and inventions. For years, his institute thrived. It provided information and research funds for many people and organizations. It was open to the public so anyone could look at the tanks of fish or skeleton of a whale on display. However, forty-five years later, the institute was in trouble.

Albert was enthusiastic, but his son Louis was not interested. He did not bother with upkeep, scientists left, labs deteriorated, and much of the equipment was sold. Tourists still came to see the skeletons and preserved specimens of marine creatures, but there was nothing new and no forward motion. It was Prince Rainier, Louis's son, who took on the challenge of restoring the once great Oceanographic Institute.

Prince Albert I ruled Monaco from 1889 until his death in 1922. He had a great interest in science and founded the Oceanographic Institute to support research and exploration.

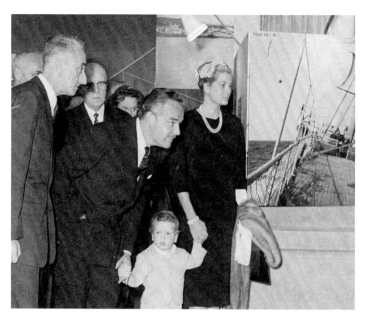

This 1960 photograph shows Cousteau giving a tour of the Oceanographic Institute to Prince Rainier of Monaco, his wife Princess Grace, and their son Prince Albert.

The Popularity of Underwater Diving

Prince Rainier counted himself among the thousands of divers who used Cousteau's aqualung. By 1960, there were an estimated 350,000 licensed divers around the world. Every year, the numbers increased as more people enjoyed using Cousteau's invention. In America, the aqualung was called a scuba. *Time* magazine—in one of the many articles they published about Cousteau—hypothesized about diving's appeal for so many people: "With no need to compete or excel, the skin diver can choose a way to have fun beneath the surface that suits his nerve and pocketbook."

Scuba in America

Another common name for the aqualung—especially in America—is scuba. This stands for self-contained underwater breathing apparatus. It means that a diver can carry everything that he or she needs in one unit.

Scuba diving was so popular by the late 1950s that it played an important role on the television show *Sea Hunt*. The sport even had its own stars, such as Zale Perry. She was a pioneer scuba diver who set a record for deepest dive by a woman—209 feet in 1954—and was one of the first female diving instructors. Perry is the author of a book on the history of scuba diving in America—*The Human History of Sports Diving*—and is a founder of the Underwater Photographic Society.

People are now learning how to use an aqualung system in town pools. The sport is open to almost anyone who can afford the classes. There are organized dives in rivers and lakes, along tropical coasts, and arctic ice sheets. A new record for underground cave diving was set in 2005—to a depth of 900 feet in South Africa.

The popularity of scuba diving has only increased over the years. It is a sport enjoyed the world over. This 1998 photograph shows a woman petting a dolphin in the Bahamas.

CHAPTER 8

The Conshelf Experiments

*It is the first time in twenty years of diving that
I really have time to see.*

— *Albert Falco*

Cousteau "decided from the beginning that those on board were companions in the adventure, whatever their jobs might be." The *Calypso* did not have separate areas for officers, scientists, and crew. Everyone lived, worked, and ate together. "No one shouted orders, and no one wore anything resembling a uniform." Mealtimes, in particular, were lively occasions when they "discussed plans, made decisions, and learned from each other."

Even though she rarely appeared on camera, his wife was a constant presence on board the *Calypso*. In fact, she logged more hours aboard the research vessel than anyone else, including Jacques. She was there for more than support, though. She pitched in like any other member of the crew, acting as "supply officer, nurse, assistant cook and sonarman."

Jacques and Simone on the *Calypso* in 1959. Simone considered the *Calypso* home. She spent more time on board the ship than anyone else, including her husband.

Oceanographic Advancements

On June 15, 1957, all of France had the opportunity to see the *Calypso* team in action. The television special *Live from the Sea Floor* followed the *Calypso* as it visited sunken ships—the Roman wreck near Grand Congloué and another closer to Marseilles. As expected, the show was a popular event.

Cousteau and his companies were constantly designing and testing new equipment, some of them taking years to develop. The diving saucer, for instance, was finally ready for its first test run in March 1957. It would take another sixteen months before it was ready for regular use. Referred to as the SP-350, the diving saucer was the world's first two-person mini-sub and was soon a vital part of *Calypso* research. "It completely changed the character of underwater exploration, affording for the first time man's active presence in waters as deep as 1,150 feet."

Cousteau is shown sitting in an early version of his diving saucer. The photo was taken in 1959 during an Oceanographic Conference in New York City.

In 1958, Cousteau also designed the *Troika*—a sled that could be towed at depths of 25,000 feet or more and had automatic Edgerton cameras and flashguns attached to it. The next year, Cousteau took movies filmed with the *Troika* to the First International Oceanographic Congress held in New York City. Oceanographers and marine scientists from around the world were impressed by images of dark cliffs and valleys along the ocean floor.

As the *Calypso* sailed into New York Harbor for the congress, they were met with "an escort of hooting tugboats, waterworks from the city's fireboats, and ear-piercing sirens from both ships and docks." During their stay, Cousteau met with scientists and journalists to discuss the *Calypso*'s unique role in oceanography and what he planned to do next.

In the early 1960s, the United States and the USSR were in a race to see who would be the first to put a man on the moon. President Kennedy even predicted that America would achieve this goal before the end of the decade. While many people were looking to the stars, Jacques Cousteau continued looking to the sea. He believed that people could learn much more about themselves by looking closer to home.

Cousteau appeared on the cover of *Time* magazine on March 28, 1960. The article introduced Cousteau to millions of Americans.

He often wondered what would happen if humans could live underwater. How would living on the ocean floor for a week or more affect the human body and mind? Would these people look at the ocean surrounding them differently if it was their home, too? So began Jacques Cousteau's most ambitious project to date.

Conshelf I

On September 14, 1962 at 12:20 p.m., two aquanauts, or oceanauts (opposed to astronauts who went to outer space), dived into the Mediterranean Sea. They were Albert Falco and Claude Wesley, and they made there way to a dwelling place that was near the coast of Marseille and located in waters about thirty-five feet down. They would be *living* in their new underwater home for a week.

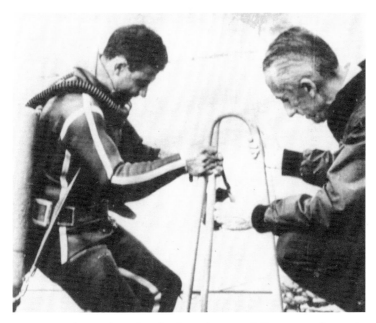

Cousteau watches as Falco and Wesley descend into Conshelf I on September 14, 1962. In order to document everything, Cousteau also photographed the men as they lived below.

The aquanauts' home was called Conshelf I, and it was based on designs by Dr. George Bond, an American inventor. The cylindrical structure, which resembled a long tube, was seventeen feet long and eight feet high at its peak. It rested on an underwater plain called the continental shelf—hence, its name Conshelf.

It took more than a year of planning and designing before Conshelf I became a reality. Cousteau was involved—and in charge—every step of the way. He brought along a film crew to record each new development and held press conferences throughout the aquanauts' weeklong stay. Newspapers all over the world covered the story of the two men living in the ocean. The experiment proved to be emotionally exhausting for them, but it was an incredible experience.

The two men had a view like no other. They could quietly observe the fish from their solitude in Conshelf I without disturbing the sea creatures. "It is the first time in 20 years of diving that I really have time to see," Falco said.

They could quietly observe the fish from their solitude in Conshelf I without disturbing the sea creatures.

It was not an entirely pleasant experience, though. Falco, in particular, had trouble with the close space and being constantly observed. He had dreams that someone was strangling him and was "obsessed with a ridiculous idea: What if the air pressure falls and the water comes in?"

Cousteau considered the experiment a great success, so they "decided on a lengthier experiment with more men and with a deeper extension of the settlement." It was not Cousteau's curiosity alone that fueled these missions. He had funding from gas and petroleum companies that wondered if miners could live

Continental Shelf

The continental shelf is a ridge or platform that juts out from each continental coast below see level. The soil on this shelf is rich in mineral deposits, sea life, and fossils. Since the last ice age ended, about 20,000 years ago, dirt and silt have been building up along this ridge. Almost everything that washes off land and into the sea rests on the shelf, providing rich soil and food for plant life. In turn, the fertile plants bring in more sea life making the continental shelf near France the perfect place for Cousteau's observatory station.

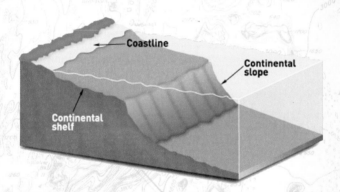

This graphic illustrates how the sea floor descends from the coastline, forming the continental shelf, before dropping suddenly to greater ocean depths.

on the sea floor. They also hoped that Cousteau and his team might locate valuable mineral deposits during their stay.

Cousteau found another source of funding for this second and much more elaborate and costly project. After his great success with the film *The Silent World* and the popularity of his television specials, a movie studio gave Cousteau money to film in Conshelf II.

Conshelf II

A team of five men set up headquarters in Conshelf II in the summer of 1963. This time, they were in the Red Sea, near the coast of Sudan. The main section of Conshelf II was shaped like a dome and was called Starfish House. It had sleeping quarters for eight, a lab, and a film developing room. The setup provided a much easier life than the first attempt within Conshelf I. Even though Starfish House had a kitchen, many of the meals were prepared on the surface and delivered to the aquanauts daily. It was during this time that Jacques and Simone celebrated their twenty-sixth wedding anniversary with the Conshelf II crew, thirty-five feet beneath the surface of the sea. They strapped on their aqualungs and dove to the shelter to join the crew for dinner.

The setup provided a much easier life than the first attempt within Conshelf I.

There was also a second smaller structure called Deep Cabin that sat eighty-five feet below sea level. Unfortunately, this was a much less enjoyable place to stay. It could only fit two men, and it was very hot inside as the air conditioner did not work properly. Even though the conditions were not ideal, Cousteau felt it was important to experiment with different environments.

They used DS-2, their latest diving saucer, to move between the two dwellings. The DS-2 was so small that it could maneuver like a fish. It did not use rudders or propellers like an ordinary submarine. The DS-2 used jets of air to propel through the water. By adjusting the direction of these powerful air streams, it could be moved easily in any desired direction.

Just as he did with Conshelf I, Cousteau always had cameras

This still photograph made from *World Without Sun*—a film Cousteau made about their time in Conshelf II—shows a diver swimming past one of the structures.

ready. The cameras followed the Conshelf inhabitants as they moved through the ocean in the diving saucer or swam with their aqualungs. The men were filmed relaxing, playing chess, or enjoying coffee together. They seemed like men going about their daily lives just as millions of others did each day. The only difference, of course, was that their work, play, and rest took place underwater.

Cousteau made a documentary of this time called *World Without Sun* (1964). It was an extraordinary view into an unknown world. The cameras saw what the men saw. Everyone who watched the film had a chance to experience life in the ocean.

Conshelf III

When Jacques established Conshelf III in 1965, he sent six men, including his twenty-four-year-old son Philippe, to live for three weeks at a depth of about 330 feet below the surface. This time, Conshelf III was back in the Mediterranean Sea near a small island called Île du Levant. The venture was a success—much like Conshelf I and Conshelf II—with the men living and working underwater with little trouble. Although no major scientific discoveries were made during this final attempt, Conshelf III had a significant affect on Cousteau's career.

Conshelf III was more elaborate than the other Conshelfs, so Cousteau had to spend much of his own money on it. Rather

In 1964 Cousteau presents the designs for Conshelf III to the media. It would be another year before the structure was built and inhabited.

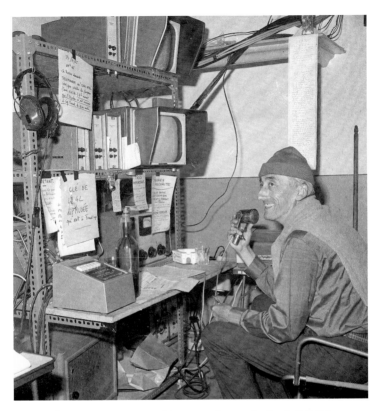

In September 1965, Cousteau sits at his command center for Conshelf III. Using television cameras and radios, he kept in close contact with the men.

than making a feature film to release in the theaters, Cousteau sold the footage—largely shot by Philippe—to the National Geographic Society, which aired it as a television special for American audiences. The special received great critical acclaim and large ratings. It helped pay some of Cousteau's bills from Conshelf III, but more importantly, it opened up new doors for him. In a very short time, Jacques Cousteau would be a television star.

CHAPTER 9

A Resident of the Sea

*We have been overexploiting the sea, dumping
great quantities of waste into it as though it were
both an inexhaustible bounty and a sewer.*

On February 18, 1967, Jacques Cousteau stood on
the deck of his beloved ship, the *Calypso*. He was
surrounded by journalists, news cameras, and
photographers. They had all traveled to Monaco to
hear Cousteau make an important announcement.

Cousteau and crew were about to depart on their
longest and most significant mission yet. The *Calypso* was

Cousteau, pictured
here preparing for
another dive in 1965,
wanted first-hand
knowledge of the
world around him.
He wanted to capture
as much as he could
before the oceans
were damaged
beyond repair.

leaving on a four-year expedition to explore and film the oceans. He explained that the world was changing, and he felt that pollution and over-fishing were destroying the oceans. Cousteau recounted how over the past two years, the *Calypso* had sailed the Mediterranean conducting tests on underwater **seismic** activity and laying pipeline along the ocean

> *The* Calypso *was leaving on a four-year expedition to explore and film the oceans.*

floor—the same areas where he had first experienced the joy of underwater life in the late 1930s. Now, he could see that the waters and marine life had suffered. There were fewer fish, the coral was depleting, and plant life was in decline. Cousteau wanted to record everything—capture this fragile system on film—before it disappeared.

The Undersea World of Jacques Cousteau

This entire adventure would be filmed and broadcast on American television in a twelve-part series. Cousteau was given complete control of *The Undersea World of Jacques Cousteau*. He would decide where the *Calypso* traveled to, what they filmed, and the topic of each episode. The television series paid the expenses so Cousteau did not have to worry about money. He could concentrate on exploration and filming. Cousteau wanted few distractions from his mission as he planned "to essentially become real residents of the sea."

Cousteau loved movies but he understood the power of television, and he was ready to find a larger audience. "You know that on one evening, thirty-five to forty million people are going to see dolphins," he said. Soon, whenever people thought of the undersea world, they would also think of Jacques Cousteau.

Before heading out, the *Calypso* needed renovations. Many modifications were made since 1950, but now she needed a complete overhaul. Engines, smokestack, and hull were cleaned and repaired. New radio, sonar, and radar systems were installed. They replaced the false nose with another, roomier version to make observation easier. They had new mini-subs—the P-500 or *Sea Flea*—and a larger two-man sub, which required new storage space and a launching pad.

Cousteau demonstrates the *Sea Flea*'s many features to the French press in 1967. The mini-sub could dive to a depth of about 150 feet below sea level.

As usual, Simone Cousteau performed multiple roles aboard the *Calypso*, and Frederic Dumas was chief diver. Jacques and Simone's youngest son, Philippe, joined the crew as a camera operator. Their older son Jean-Michel only joined *Calypso* expeditions occasionally. Instead, he left the "family business" and went to architecture school.

For his television series, Cousteau wanted to have scientists for each episode because he knew that he was sometimes criticized for his lack of formal training. He was not a scientist or biologist and wanted to get all the facts right. While filming the television series, experts in different fields were brought on board the *Calypso*. If the subject were dolphins, a marine biologist was available to answer any questions. An archeologist was on hand during dives exploring sunken ships.

Over the next several months, they traveled the Indian and the Atlantic Oceans and the Caribbean Sea. They stopped along the way to film whatever interested them. They shot footage of thousands of penguins on St. Croix Island, near the South African coast. The crew "watched and filmed these fascinating birds as they went about their daily parades, games, and rituals." Cousteau and his team swam with sea lions and dolphins, searched for sunken ships in the Caribbean Sea, and traveled

All types of wildlife, like these South African penguins captured in this 2002 photograph, became popular topics for Cousteau's television programs.

along South American rivers to Lake Titicaca in Brazil. They even used dolphins as crewmembers—strapping remote cameras on them and enlisting them as camera operators. All of these adventures were filmed for later television episodes.

An Instant Hit

The first episode of *The Undersea World of Jacques Cousteau* aired in January 1968. The episode was simply called "Sharks," and it made for very exciting viewing. The sight of men swimming with sharks amazed the television audience. Camera operators were lowered into the water in a cage and held steady while sharks swept past them, brushing against the steel bars. One very brave crewmember even rode on the back of a whale shark. Philippe Cousteau summed up their adventure with these creatures by saying, "It was good that we finished without trouble because I think we were getting overconfident."

Underwater cages were often the only protection Cousteau's divers and cameramen had against dangerous predators. The one shown here was used by the *Calypso* crew when working in the Persian Gulf in 1985.

Although episodes of *The Undersea World of Jacques Cousteau* were scheduled to air over a five-year span, the series lasted nine years. The shows were educational and informative, but Cousteau wanted them to be seen as something more. No one had seen anything like it before. Audiences were watching an exotic and sometimes dangerous world up close—in the comfort of their home. Most nature shows were quiet and reserved. Cousteau's show was lively and exciting. The viewers felt a part of the action. As Cousteau once said, "We are not documentary. We are adventure film."

In 1972, Cousteau and his *Calypso* crew visited Antarctica. It is a magnificent and fragile continent that is mostly covered by a permanent sheet of ice. It is the home of penguins, walruses, fish, and even some small plants. To show the sheets

Cousteau visited Antarctica in 1972 and featured some of the animals living there. This undated photograph shows the coastline and a whale skeleton along the shore.

of ice from below, the team dived under the thick frozen layer to get an underwater perspective. They also used a helicopter and hot air balloon to fly over the land. All of these sights and adventures were turned into the film, *Voyage to the End of the World*.

Antarctica can also be a harsh and dangerous environment. Temperatures can drop to a deathly -80°F and winds can whip up to one hundred miles per hour. In the winter months, the seas around the continent are covered with ice. Anything in this area during this time risks being crushed as sheets of ice move over the water. The poor *Calypso* almost suffered such a fate, and she "certainly bore the scars of her arduous Antarctic expedition . . ." When they returned from the "end of the world," Cousteau's beloved ship spent almost a year being repaired.

The Cousteau Society

When Cousteau set out on his odyssey to film the oceans and their wild life, he wanted to capture their beauty to show the world what it would lose unless care was taken. Cousteau was surprised to discover the level of destruction that already existed. He was watching Earth's riches disappear before his very eyes. "We have been overexploiting the sea," he said in a 1970 interview with *Time* magazine, "dumping great quantities of waste into it as though it were both an inexhaustible bounty and a sewer."

Cousteau stepped to the forefront of the environmentalist movement. He used *The Undersea World* as a platform to discuss environmental issues and started attending conferences and giving interviews on the subject. Cousteau was adamant that there was no time to waste. "Monitoring the sea must begin immediately so we can assess our impact." As a result, he founded the Cousteau Society in 1973.

Through his Society, Cousteau worked to clean up the refuse left at the bottom of the sea by thoughtless people. This c. 2003 photograph shows a pile of toilets found in the Red Sea.

The initial goal of the society was education. Cousteau believed that if people knew the state of the oceans, they would do something to help. *The Undersea World of Jacques Cousteau* was the best advertisement. The society pledged itself "to the protection and improvement of the quality of life." Within a year, they had 120,000 members.

> *Cousteau believed that if people knew the state of the oceans, they would do something to help.*

The society was so successful that Cousteau made it the central office for all his work. It was a nonprofit organization, so Jacques never received a salary from the society. All of the money earned by membership fees and sponsorships funded *Calypso* expeditions, explorations, the society offices in the United States (its headquarters were in Norfolk, Virginia) and France, and any promotional costs.

Cousteau and the *Calypso* still accepted work and contracts with other organizations but only if he considered them important. In 1975, he took on just such a project when the *Calypso* was used to test satellite equipment for **NASA**. Landsat 1 (Land Remote-Sensing Satellite) and Landsat 2 took photographs from space of the coral reef near the Bahamas while the *Calypso* took sonar and visual readings of the same area. NASA wanted to know if satellites could accurately map from space. By comparing their data with the information the *Calypso* collected, it was determined that satellites were indeed effective mapping tools.

Cousteau met many world leaders while working as an explorer and environmentalist. In this photo, he sits with future president Jimmy Carter at a United Nations conference on nuclear energy in 1976.

The *Britannic*

The *Britannic* belonged to the White Star line of luxury cruisers, and was a sister ship to the *Titanic*—designed to transport travelers across the Atlantic Ocean. However, the *Britannic* took on a new role during World War I. She became a hospital ship for the British navy, touring combat zones and picking up the sick and wounded. The ship struck a German mine on November 21, 1916. Miraculously, only thirty men lost their lives and more than a thousand were saved.

The German government claimed the *Britannic* was spying on the area and was not an innocent hospital ship at all. When Cousteau and his crew examined the ship, they could find no evidence of spying or surveillance equipment. It was Cousteau's opinion that the *Britannic* was on a humanitarian—not a spy—mission.

The *Britannic*—pictured above—was a sister ship to the *Titanic*. Built around the same time, they were initially designed as luxury ocean liners.

In the fall of that year, the *Calypso* sailed for another year-long journey. It was heading to the Aegean Sea—located north of the Mediterranean—to search for lost civilizations. It would be another long year of underwater excavation as the crew unearthed ships, pottery, and even a submerged harbor that was approximately 3,000 years old. While surveying the area in a diving saucer, they also located the wreck of the *Britannic*, a British hospital ship that sank in 1916 during World War I. They were the first men to examine the wreck, and they shared this exciting find with their television audience.

Cousteau's campaign to preserve the oceans received official recognition in May 1977. He was appointed Secretary General of International Committee for the Scientific Exploration of the Mediterranean. His first official act was to assign the *Calypso* the job of monitoring the entire Mediterranean. The crew would collect data on pollution and erosion levels in the ocean by taking "samples of water, sediments, plankton, and other organisms on the shores of twelve Mediterranean countries." Cousteau's years of hard work were rewarded in 1977 when the United Nations awarded him the International Environmental Prize.

Philippe Cousteau, Jacques's youngest son, joined his father on most of *Calypso*'s expeditions. He worked as a pilot, a cameraman and, of course, a diver.

Tragedy Strikes Home

No matter what he was doing or where he was in the world, Cousteau was always with his family—in particular, his wife, Simone. They had a house in Monaco and an apartment in Paris, but they were often traveling together aboard the *Calypso*. Jean-Michel, his eldest son, worked for his father for years but left to work as an architect. It was Philippe who was always at his father's side.

Philippe worked with him on all of his television documentaries and was a vital part of the *Calypso* crew. Much like his father, Philippe was active in every part of the business and rarely slowed down. He was a diver, pilot, camera operator, producer, and writer. He was always trying out new equipment, taking a camera to new depths, or searching for new treasures to unearth.

Philippe worked with him on all of his television documentaries and was a vital part of the Calypso *crew.*

June 28, 1979, seemed like any other day in their lives as Philippe took to the air in a small plane. The *Flying Calypso* had recently been repaired and Philippe wanted to make sure it was working properly. His pregnant wife and young daughter were waiting for him on shore. Philippe was only gone for a short time when they received word that his plane had crashed into the sea. Rescue teams raced out immediately, but it took two days to locate the wreckage. Philippe was killed instantly when his plane hit the water.

In public, Cousteau sounded stoically accepting of his son's death. "That is fate. We must accept it and move on." In private, however, the entire family was devastated, especially Jacques. Philippe was supposed to inherit Cousteau's lifework. He had

Part of Philippe Cousteau's plane is pulled from the water on June 29, 1979, after it crashed near Lisbon, Portugal, killing Cousteau's youngest son instantly.

expected his son to take over the business and continue a life of exploration and film. Now, Jacques was at a loss.

A few months after Philippe's death, Jacques sent out a letter to the members of the Cousteau Society. He wrote about the joy of introducing his son to diving and the sea when Philippe was a young boy. Cousteau also spoke of the pride he felt as a father whenever his son had something wonderful to show him—like the time he watched Philippe pilot a plane. "I looked at you, my guide in the sky as I had been your guide in the sea—I saw

> *"I looked at you, my guide in the sky as I had been your guide in the sea . . ."*

your shining face, proud to have something to give back to me, and I smiled, because I knew that pursuing rainbows in your plane, you would always seek after the vanishing shapes of a better world."

After Philippe's death, Jean-Michel came back to the family business. He took over where his younger brother left off. He produced documentaries for his father and worked to promote the Cousteau Society and their environmentalist cause. As hard as it was for all of them, they continued their important work.

Jean-Michel's work with the Cousteau Society took on many aspects. This 1981 photograph shows him at an auction to raise money for the society.

CHAPTER 10

The Odyssey Continues

To improve the condition of man is the purpose of life, and the goal of science is to make people more happy. I film it because I love it.

Even though Cousteau lived so much of his life in front of cameras, there were still things that he kept hidden. While Jacques tried to make Simone, Philippe, and later Jean-Michel a part of every story aboard the *Calypso*, he kept a big secret from his fans: Cousteau had a growing second family. Francine Triplet, a woman forty years younger than Jacques, gave birth to his daughter Diane in 1980. Another child, son Pierre-Yves, was born in 1982. Their existence was not revealed for many years. Having such a large secret is amazing when one considers how often Cousteau was in the spotlight.

Discovering Life Above the Water

The Cousteau Society regularly published books, and Cousteau continued to produce television shows. In the late 1970s, his show was called *The Cousteau Odyssey*. This time, each program was treated like a

Francine Triplet Cousteau, pictured here in a 1997 photograph, was a flight attendant when she met Cousteau. Her relationship with Cousteau was not revealed to the public until the early 1990s.

feature film rather than a television show. The camera crew on board the *Calypso* shot a tremendous amount of film—sometimes fifty or sixty times more than what they needed—and edited it down to a one-hour television program. Each episode had a narrator, sometimes Cousteau himself, and music written specifically for that show. So, even though there was an established formula to the shows—same introduction, same crew—each episode was unique. Jacques did not take his audience for granted. He assumed they were like him and always wanted more—something new, something different.

Jacques and his team documented more than ocean life. Cameras followed the crew of the *Calypso* as they discovered the beauty and mystery of this planet—on land and in the sea. They visited remote islands, journeyed on rivers, and filmed exotic animals and plants. By showing the world above and under the water, Cousteau was reminding his viewers how one affects the other.

Cameras followed the crew of the Calypso as they discovered the beauty and mystery of this planet—on land and in the sea.

In the episode called "Clipperton: The Island that Time Forgot," the *Calypso* crew visited this tiny island near the coast of Mexico. Their cameras caught the lives of sea birds on nests, raising their young. They followed crabs living along the rocks as the crabs sidled into the nests, stealing the birds' eggs. The audience watched as the crabs retreated quickly to their rocky hideaways. Even though these creatures were not much bigger than a man's hand, the camera was so close that the picture filled the screen.

Through his television show, Cousteau made nature approachable. He also made something that was possibly scary, fascinating. He was very careful not to label nature as

Clipperton Island was deserted when Cousteau filmed his television documentary. No one had lived on the island for more than sixty years—not since the end of World War I.

good or bad. There were no heroes and no villains. Cousteau wanted to show the natural world in all its beauty but also that it could be frightening or harsh. He felt that if humans could understand nature, they would come to respect it. "Our films have only one ambition—to show the truth about nature and give people the wish to know more. I do not stand as a scientist giving dry explanations. I'm an honest observer."

The *Calypso* crew always looked like they had the best job in the world. They worked hard, constantly diving and diving some more. They faced storms and broken equipment and disruptive sea creatures. There were dolphins that did not cooperate while filming and sharks that came too close. Almost always, though, when the camera caught the crew in a quiet moment, they were smiling.

In an episode titled "Diving for Roman Plunder," the crew was filmed exploring the sunken wreck of a Roman ship. They pulled up vases, urns, and plates from the ocean floor. Remarkably, many of the pieces were in fairly good shape—one of the benefits of remaining undisturbed for centuries. That night, on the deck of the *Calypso*, the men enjoyed a Roman feast. Just as they did at Port Calypso almost thirty years earlier, they dressed in togas. The crew took their job seriously—but not themselves.

Not all of their adventures were based solely on science or history. Their curiosity extended to the mysterious and unknown. In one of his most popular episodes, Cousteau went in search of the lost island of Atlantis. The likelihood of finding the island was very, very small—almost impossible some might say—but Cousteau never gave up thinking that anything was possible. Even the fantastic and mystical might prove to be true.

Cousteau never lost his sense of curiosity or excitement about exploring the undersea world. This 1974 photograph shows him smiling and happy while preparing for another dive.

Atlantis

The island of Atlantis first appeared in Greek mythology and in the writings of ancient Greece. Legend has it that Atlantis was a highly advanced civilization. Some say it was a city in perfect harmony with advancements such as cars, airplanes, and computers. Aristotle, a Greek philosopher and scientist, wrote about it, claiming it disappeared in an earthquake. No one knows when it disappeared or if it ever existed in the first place—most scholars believe it is a land based more in fiction than fact. That does not mean that Atlantis had no roots in reality. These stories might have been based on a civilization or city that actually disappeared. The most popular theory locates Atlantis near the upper-west side of Africa, although others think the remains of Atlantis might be found in Alaska or Antarctica.

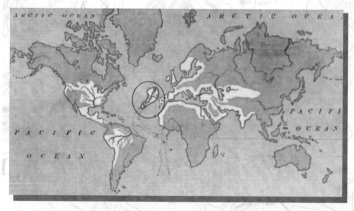

The title of this 1882 map is The Empire of Atlantis. The mythological island (circled here) is in the Atlantic Ocean, near the coast of northern Africa.

Looking at Wind Power

If Cousteau was going to ask other people to change their lives to help the environment, he knew he should do the same. He questioned how much he was contributing to the problem with his ships and submarines. They all required a great deal of fuel. He started to investigate alternative sources of energy.

He needed to find something that was both powerful and in constant abundance. Cousteau looked around him and came up with the perfect solution. Aside from water, what was the one thing that was always nearby, especially out on the high seas? Wind! On the ocean, there was a never-ending supply of wind.

Jacques and his team at the Cousteau Society started work on the turbosail—a tall tower with a windmill blade on top. The technology was very old. Wind power and windmills have been used for centuries— long before electricity, oil, or gas.

Aside from water, what was the one thing that was always nearby, especially out on the high seas? Wind!

Cousteau wanted the turbosail to power a boat like a very powerful sail would. Engineers with the Cousteau Society attached two turbosails to the *Alcyone*, another ship in the Cousteau Society fleet. The *Alcyone*, like the *Calypso* was named after a character from Greek mythology. Alcyone was the daughter of the Greek god of wind, which made the name a very appropriate choice for a ship equipped with a turbosail.

Although the ship looked very awkward—like it might tip the ship over—it was actually quite steady. The turbosail not only cut down the ship's use of other fuel by thirty percent, it also provided an effective method for collecting energy. Although this new device was not a perfect solution—and it was used on only one ship—like so many of Cousteau's projects, he just wanted to prove that it could be done.

Cousteau's wind-powered boat the *Alcyone* houses the turbosail towers on her deck. Wind is collected inside these stacks and converted to energy to fuel the ship.

CHAPTER 11

The Final Journey Home

*. . . Captain Cousteau showed us both the
importance of the world's oceans and the beauty
that lies within.*

—*President Bill Clinton*

ousteau showed few signs of slowing down. On
the occasion of his seventy-fifth birthday, he did
not have a quiet party with friends and family. Oh no,
not Jacques! He was the subject of a television special
called *Jacques Cousteau: The First 75 Years*. It featured clips
from his years as a filmmaker and interviews with friends,
colleagues, and admirers. There was also a concert held in
his honor. It was a fitting tribute but it was a little strange
to see Jacques Cousteau sitting quietly during
the show. Normally, he was a man of action
and movement.

Of course, he did not sit still for long. As
part of his ongoing environmental campaign,
he wanted to show the disintegration of parts
of the world. The Cousteau Society now
boasted a membership of 250,000, and
Jacques wanted to take full advantage of this
support. So, in 1990, he returned to

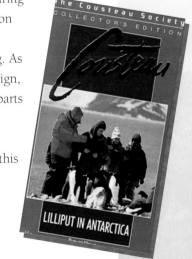

The Cousteau Society still supports campaigns
to conserve Antarctica. Cousteau's work on
television—*Lilliput in Antarctica*, in particular—
played an important part in their program.

Antarctica, retracing an expedition he had made almost twenty years earlier.

When Jacques returned to Antarctica in 1990 he brought six eleven-year-old school children from six continents with him. It was Jacques's symbolic way of bringing the world together, and *Lilliput in Antarctica* documented this trip. Through this television special, he wanted everyone to see how much the continent had changed in twenty years, and how the ecosystem, with ice melting, was in danger.

Upon returning to France, Cousteau immediately started a petition to save the southern continent. He wanted it preserved as a "natural reserve." It was one of his favorite places, and he wanted to protect it from further harm.

The Loss of a Life Partner

In 1990, Cousteau suffered a terrible loss. Simone, his wife of fifty-three years, passed away. Throughout all of the television shows, Simone was on board the *Calypso* but avoided the spotlight. Cousteau said she preferred the crow's nest where she would sit high above the deck, watching for whales and the crew below.

Her nickname was *La Bergère*—the Shepherdess—because she took care of everyone. According to Jan Cousteau, Philippe's widow, she was "mother, healer, nurse and psychiatrist" to

Simone, photographed with her husband in 1952 at their home in Toulon, never sought the spotlight. She may have preferred a supporting role in the Cousteau odyssey, but she was invaluable to all his work.

Ecosystem

An ecosystem is any portion of an environment that works as one complete unit. A pond, for instance, is one ecosystem. All of the plants, animals, and insects living around the pond rely on each other for survival. If one element is damaged or removed, the entire system is affected. Many tiny ecosystems fit into larger ones. The Earth, with every one thing affecting the other, is a gigantic ecosystem.

This little pond represents an ecosystem on a small scale. In it, the plants, animals, insects, and water source rely on each other to sustain life.

the *Calypso* crew. Simone was always ready to provide whatever was needed. She was also a diver and joined her husband on many trips below. Simone was a good match for Jacques. She was curious about the world around her and patient enough for a husband who was rushing to see it all.

Over the years, Simone's influential family had been a great help to Cousteau, especially in the earlier years of their marriage. It was her father who had contacted Emile Gagnon about Cousteau's aqualung project. In addition, until he was able to forge his own connections, Simone had introduced him to powerful people who donated money or supplies to his next round of expeditions. Her contribution to her husband's work was immeasurable. Simone was cremated, and her ashes were scattered over the ocean near their home in Monaco.

Environmental Work Continues

As always, Cousteau continued. In June 1991, he married Francine Triplet, the mother of his youngest children. Francine quickly stepped into her new role as the wife of Jacques Cousteau.

He was now producing fewer television specials, and diving became more difficult. In 1995, he told the *Los Angeles Times* that, "At my age I don't go diving in ice-cold water anymore. But if the water is warm or lukewarm then, yes, I go with pleasure!" However, his work as an environmentalist continued to increase.

Jacques and Francine Cousteau enjoy a happy moment in Cannes in April 1995. Francine joined her husband in his work, taking on a more public role than Simone.

The environmental movement was growing stronger each year as people became aware of the serious issues at stake. Cousteau was the elder statesman—a wise man with decades of experience in the cause. He was traveling almost fulltime, speaking at the Earth Summit and the United Nations Conference on Environment and Development, in 1992. He also accepted a seat on a United Nations Advisory Board on Sustainable Development as one of a select group of people assigned to monitor new environmental issues that may arise.

Sustainable Development

Sustainable development is a process by which the needs of all humans are adequately met, but in a way that will still ensure the environment for future generations. There are no set rules for sustainable development.

Each individual should be asking: How will we survive if we consume too much of Earth's natural resources—trees, oil, gas—and what will happen if we allow the air and water to become polluted? What will be left for the future generations? Earth is like a giant ecosystem—what we do today will affect what happens tomorrow.

In maintaining a sustainable environment, one must consider deforestation and the replenishing of trees. Deforestation can be seen in this photograph of Beavercreek, Oregon, where trees have been clearcut.

Family Difficulties

Working at a steady pace, Jacques continued his functions with the Cousteau Society, but trouble was brewing in his family. Since Philippe's death, Jean-Michel had been working alongside his father producing programs and running the Cousteau Society. They often disagreed—as two strong-willed people will—but always managed to get the job done. After Simone's death, though, it was much more difficult to come to agreements. They each had their own ideas about what to do next. They finally broke their professional ties in 1992 with Jean-Michel leaving to seek other interests, including founding the Ocean Futures Society.

Unfortunately, their disagreements did not end there. In 1995, Cousteau sued his son over using the name Cousteau for a beach resort.

It was an eco-friendly resort on the island of Fiji. Guests would learn about responsible tourism and ethical diving practices. Since his father's invention of the aqualung, divers disturbing fish and plant life and tampering with coral reef had caused a lot of damage. The resort provided lectures and had experts on hand to discuss the problems in the sea and what could be done about it.

Nevertheless, Jacques felt that using the Cousteau name was misleading. People would think that he was involved when in fact he strongly opposed the resort. The Cousteau Society was a

Jean-Michel's resort in Fiji remains a popular tourist destination. It offers eco-friendly activities and on-staff marine biologists to answer guests' questions.

Ecotourism

The environmentalist movement has grown considerably since Cousteau's day. As people have become more aware of pollution and over-consumption, they have also become more mindful of how the way they live and work affects the environment. They are seeking out alternative methods of energy, food production, and even methods of travel.

Ecotourism follows the belief that there is an ethical and responsible way to see the world. It means visiting places that work to conserve their environment, support local communities, and maintain a goal of sustainable development. Or it could mean that travelers make sure they don't disturb the environment they visit—that they leave the area just as they found it. Some places, like Jean-Michel Cousteau's resort in Fiji, have an educational component. The visitors can attend seminars, learn about the area, or even work with residents to improve the area. These resorts teach that it is important to leave a place better than when visitors found it.

Other countries are beginning to offer eco-friendly tourism. Pictured here are the rainforests of Costa Rica where many resorts offer vacation spots for people who want to travel in a responsible way.

nonprofit organization. It was funded mainly through membership fees and donations. Cousteau claimed it would harm the society's reputation if people thought it was associated with a moneymaking resort.

This was a difficult time for the family, as the legal battle threatened to tear them apart. In the end, it was decided that the resort could go ahead as planned as long as Jean-Michel's full name was clearly displayed. There must be no doubt that it was Jean-Michel's business, not Jacques's.

In 1996, Cousteau sustained another great loss—his beloved ship. The *Calypso* sank in Singapore Harbor when a barge ran into her. Even though the Cousteau Society had other ships in use—most noticeably, the *Alcyone*—the sinking was a terrible shock for Jacques. The *Calypso* had been his mainstay—his home and office for more than forty years. Almost every important journey was taken aboard the *Calypso*. She was a beloved character from all of his films, books, and television shows, and she would be missed by millions of Cousteau's fans and admirers. As Jacques himself said, "She's an old ship but she's a darling." The *Calypso* was raised from the bottom of the harbor and towed back to France.

Tragedy struck in 1996 when the *Calypso* sank after being hit by a barge. In happier times, Cousteau is seen smiling on board his beloved *Calypso* in July 1986.

The *Calypso's* Fame

Just how famous was Cousteau's ship? Apparently, she was famous enough to inspire a hit song. Singer John Denver released "Calypso" in 1975 and it reached number one in the charts. "Aye Calypso, the places you've been to, the things that you've shown us, the stories you tell." It was a fitting tribute to a ship that had shown us the world.

This fame, however, did not ensure a good end for the ship. The *Calypso* has sat in a state of disrepair since the day she was towed back to France from Singapore. No one can decide who officially owns her or what should be done with her. Over the years, various attempts have been made to repair and refit her with the possibility of turning the *Calypso* into a museum. Every attempt has met with opposition, though, as no one can agree on what is best for the ship. Unfortunately, this bitter battle has left the *Calypso* to slowly rot away.

Unfortunately, little was done to preserve the *Calypso* since returning it from Singapore in 1996. She has been left to slowly fall apart in a shipyard in France.

Death of a Seaman

Jacques Cousteau passed away on June 25, 1997 from heart failure at the age of eighty-seven. A memorial service was held in Notre Dame Cathedral in Paris—an honor normally reserved for heads of state, presidents, and kings. Television crews covered the mass, capturing the president of France bowing before the great man's casket. Cousteau was buried in his family's plot in Saint-André-de-Cubzac.

Following his death, the world mourned. Tributes poured in from all over the world for him, including one from President Bill Clinton, who recalled Cousteau's achievements. "Through his many documentaries, movies, and television specials, Captain Cousteau showed us both the importance of the world's oceans and the beauty that lies within. We are all far richer, and more caring, for his having shared his time on Earth with the human family."

In the years following Cousteau's death, there were many ups and downs for the family. The Cousteau Society is still

After his death, Cousteau's body was returned to his hometown of Saint-André-de-Cubzac for burial on July 3, 1997.

active, although the membership has declined since his death. It still campaigns for sound environmental practices and supports research expeditions. Jean-Michel, his children, and Philippe's children have all remained dedicated to the cause. They continue to make documentaries and crusade for the environment, still reaching millions of people over the Internet and television.

Cousteau's Legacy

So much changed over Cousteau's lifetime. He went from a time when there were few household telephones to seeing a man stand on the moon. When he was a boy, there was no television, but as a man, he became a television superstar.

Of all of Cousteau's work—his books, articles, films, environmental work, and inventions—he will best be remembered for his television documentaries. It is how he touched most people's lives. No one thinks twice anymore about photographs or films of the undersea world. Sharks, whales, penguins, dolphins, and sea turtles are welcomed into homes every week as

When he was a boy, there was no television, but as a man, he became a television superstar.

nature films and documentaries regularly air on television. Most people cannot remember a time when almost no one had ever seen a picture of a shark up close. It was Jacques Cousteau who introduced these images to the Western world.

Most people will probably never visit the Mediterranean Sea, Antarctica, or travel the Nile River, but Cousteau took them to all these places. The *Calypso* journeyed to far-off lands, captured creatures and natural wonders on film, and then brought them into homes around the world.

While certain inventions, such as the turbosail, only seemed to apply to one specific use (in this case, *the Alcyone*) and never caught on elsewhere, other inventions had a farther reach than expected. Cousteau knew the aqualung would be useful in the hands of the military and industry, including construction, but he did not predict the popularity of recreational diving. The millions of licensed scuba divers both surprised and delighted him.

Over the years, several institutions around the world recognized Cousteau's important contributions and bestowed many honors on him. Harvard University and Ghent University in Belgium presented him with honorary degrees. The United Nations awarded him the International Environmental Prize in 1977. He was admitted into the Indian Academy of Science, the French Academy, and the American National Academy of Science. Cousteau was inducted into the Television Academy of Fame and received a Founders Award from the National Academy of Television Arts and Sciences in 1987. President Ronald Reagan awarded him the Presidential Medal of Freedom in 1985—the highest American civilian award.

Cousteau is seen receiving the Presidential Medal of Freedom from President Reagan on May 23, 1985. This was only one of many tributes he received during his lifetime.

Jacques Cousteau, pictured here in 1986 aboard the *Calypso*, will be remembered as a man always searching, always curious, always exploring, always on the move.

Of course, the greatest tribute to Cousteau is when one more person is motivated into action by his work. Whenever someone watches an episode of *The Undersea World of Jacques Cousteau* or his *Odyssey* series and is moved to learn more, Jacques Cousteau lives on. When learning more leads to finding ways of doing more for the environment, Jacques Cousteau lives on.

Cousteau is proof of what one person can do when there is passion and the ability to share that passion with the world. "When one man, for whatever reason, has the opportunity to lead an extraordinary life, he has no right to keep it to himself."

Glossary

Allied forces—the combined armies of the United States, Great Britain, Russia (USSR), Canada, Australia, and other smaller forces that fought against the Axis powers of Germany, Italy, and Japan during World War II.

BCE—stands for Before Common Era: any year that occurs before year 0. For example, 326 BCE is 326 years before year 0, which marks the start of the Common Era (CE).

crow's nest—a tall mast on a ship with a basket at the top where sailors stand to scan the horizon.

diving bells—one-person-sized, bell-shaped vehicles that are lowered into the water by a cable or rope.

excavation—a site on land or in water at which earth is moved or removed to reveal objects, usually very old, that are hidden underneath.

fascist—refers to an oppressive political system led by one person with complete power that allows for no opposition.

fathoms—measured lengths used to determine depth in water. One fathom equals six feet.

flora and fauna—the Latin terms for plant and animal life.

geishas—Japanese female entertainers.

Indochina—the area of Southeast Asia that was formally a colony of France. Currently made up of Vietnam, Laos, and Cambodia.

M.—a short form for monsieur, the French word for "mister."

microcosm—a miniature world.

NASA—National Aeronautics and Space Administration: a space exploration agency run by the U.S. government.

Nazi—National Socialist Party of Germany, a fascist organization headed by Adolph Hitler.

occupation—when one country is ruled—or occupied—by another country's army.

seismic—refers to the vibrations in the ground caused by an earthquake.

snorkels—simple breathing devices for divers made up of a short tube or hose that extends from a diver's mouth to just above the surface of the water.

tour—in this instance refers to a navy assignment of a specified length.

Bibliography

Books

Cousteau, Jacques-Yves, and Diolé, Philippe. *Diving for Sunken Treasure*. London: Cassell & Company Ltd., 1972.

Cousteau, Jacques-Yves, and Diolé, Philippe. *Life and Death in a Coral Sea*. New York: Doubleday and Company, Inc., 1971.

Cousteau, Jacques, and Sivirine, Alexis. *Jacques Cousteau's Calypso*. New York: Harry N. Abrams, Inc., 1983.

Cousteau, Jacques-Yves, and Dugan, James. *The Living Sea*. New York: Harper & Row, 1963.

Cousteau, Jacques-Yves, and Dumas, Frédéric. *The Silent World*. New York: Harper and Brothers Publishing, 1953.

Cousteau, Jacques-Yves. *The Ocean World of Jacques Cousteau: Oasis in Space*. New York: World Publishing, 1973.

———. *The Ocean World of Jacques Cousteau: Outer and Inner Space*. New York: World Publishing, 1974.

———. *The Ocean World of Jacques Cousteau: Riches of the Sea*. New York: World Publishing, 1974.

———. *World Without Sun*. New York: Harper & Row, 1964.

Munson, Richard. *Cousteau: The Captain and His World*. New York: William Morrow and Company, Inc., 1989.

Periodicals

Charlier, Roger H., and Charlier Axelrod, Constance C. "Alea Semper," *Journal of Coastal Research* (September 2006).

Crook, David. "The Captain Won't Settle For Anything But Adventure," *The Los Angeles Times* (June 15, 1986).

Dugan, James. "Portrait of Homo Aquaticus," *The New York Times* (April 21, 1963).

Elnadi, Bahgat. "Jacques-Yves Cousteau: Interview," *UNESCO Courier* (November 1991).

Flowers, Charles. "The Cousteau Wars," *Cyber Diver News Network* (March 4, 2003).

Hicks, Nancy. "Cousteau's Philosophy of the Sea Helps Get Him Another Medal," *The New York Times* (October 25, 1970).

Jonas, Gerald. "Jacques Cousteau, Ocean's Impresario, Dies," *The New York Times* (June 26, 1997).

Matsumoto, Jon. "Focus: The Time of the Not-So-Ancient Mariner," *The Los Angeles Times* (November 5, 1995).

McCombs, Phil. "Cousteau: Old Man, Son, the Sea Heir-Designate Jean-Michel Stays in the Background," *The Los Angeles Times* (December 11, 1988).

Shaheen, Jack G. "The Documentary of Art: The Undersea World of Jacques Cousteau," *The Journal of Popular Culture*, Volume 21, Number 1 (Summer 1987).

Stewart-Gordon, James. "The Wet World of Jacques-Yves Cousteau," *The Saturday Evening Post* (November/December 1973).

Toufexis, Anastasia. "The Dirty Seas," *Time Magazine* (Monday, August 1, 1988).

"Calypso is Preparing to Resume Voyage," *The New York Times* (July 15, 1986).

"Poet of the Depths," *Time Magazine* (Monday, March 28, 1960).

"Into the Sea Age?" *Time Magazine* (Monday, February 9, 1953).

"New Trails," *Time Magazine* (Friday, January 19, 1968).

Web Sites and Interviews

Cousteau Society, www.cousteau.org

"Jacques Cousteau Remembered for his Common Touch," CNN Interactive: June 25, 1997.

SOURCE NOTES

The following list contains citations for the sources of the quoted material found in this book. The first and last few words of each quotation are cited and followed by its source. Complete information on referenced sources can be found in the Bibliography.

Abbreviations used are:

CCHW—*Cousteau: The Captain and His World*
CDNN—*Cyber Diver News Network*
CNN—*Cable News Network* (on-line)
C—*The Calypso*
DST—*Diving for Sunken Treasure*
JPC—*Journal of Popular Culture*
LAT—*Los Angeles Times*
LDCS—*Life and Death in the Coral Sea*
LS—*The Living Sea*
NYT—*New York Times*

OIS—*Outer and Inner Space*
CCHW—*Cousteau: The Captain and His World*
SEP—*Saturday Evening Post*
SW—*The Silent World*
TDP—*The Daring Plan to Create Fish Men*
TM—*Time*
UC—*UNESCO Courier*
WWS—*World Without Sun*

INTRODUCTION: A Life Under the Water
   PAGE 1 *"We enrich . . . of others."*: CCHW, p.255

CHAPTER 1: Birth of an Explorer
   PAGE 2 *"It happened to . . . on the sea."*: SW, p. 99
   PAGE 3 *"Henri de Montfreid's . . . and smugglers."*: LS, p.32
   PAGE 7 *"Diving in that . . . to dive."*: CCHW, p. 24
   PAGE 7 *"I spent two . . . underwater,"*: UC, November 1991
   PAGE 8 *"I created at . . . making films."*: LAT, Nov. 5, 1995
   PAGE 8 *"I was fascinated . . . devise chemicals."*: LAT, June 15, 1986
   PAGE 9 *"At Cam Ranh Bay . . . in their hands."*: UC, November 1991
   PAGE 11 *"Water is . . . medium."*: SW, p. 196
   PAGE 13 *"The sand sloped . . . to squint."*: SW p. 5
   PAGE 13 *"It happened to . . . on the sea."*: SW, p. 9

CHAPTER 2: Struggles and Success
   PAGE 14 *"It fascinated. . . . Seemed impossible."*: TM, March 28, 1960
   PAGE 23 *"above water . . . ill-fed France."*: SW. p. 7

CHAPTER 3: In Occupied France
   PAGE 24 *"When a person . . . another world."* TM, March 28, 1960
   PAGE 24 *"The Germans considered . . . were allowed."*: SEP, October/November, 1972
   PAGE 27 *"Leon Veche, machinist . . . watertight case."*: SW, p. 22
   PAGE 28 *"We could obtain . . . in a darkroom."*: SW, p. 22

CHAPTER 4: Beneath the Waves
   PAGE 32 *"No children ever . . . be revolutionized."*: SW, p. 3
   PAGE 32 *"No children ever . . . more excitement."*: SW, p. 3
   PAGE 33 *"In the center of . . . at me."*: SW, p. 6
   PAGE 34 *"I experimented with . . . and barrel rolls."*: SW. p.7
   PAGE 34 *"Diving is the . . . out of water."*: TM, March 28, 1960
   PAGE 34 *"Since that first . . . dream of flying."*: SW, p. 6
   PAGE 35 *"To the occupying . . . holiday party."*: SW, p.31
   PAGE 36 *"This proves that . . . under the sea."*: SW, p. 95

CHAPTER 5: Unexpected Dangers
   PAGE 39 *"Our worst experience . . . near Avignon."*: SW, p. 69
   PAGE 39 *"My job was . . . could do it,"*: SW, p. 52
   PAGE 39 *"Mine recovery was . . . Research Group."*: SW, p. 57
   PAGE 42 *"The peaceful water . . . wonders to me."*: SW, p. 182
   PAGE 42 *"Jean-Michel would . . . sea urchins."*: SW, p. 182

PAGE 42 *"We have always . . . a stunt man."*: SW. p. 110
PAGE 43 *"Our worst experience . . . near Avignon."*: SW, p. 69

CHAPTER 6: The *Calypso*
PAGE 50 *"We must go . . . ourselves."*: C, p. 20
PAGE 52-53 *"The bulbous chamber . . . the ship."*: C, p16
PAGE 53 *"Il faut aller voir—We must go and see for ourselves"*: C, p. 20.
PAGE 54 *"from fees from . . . television specials."*: C, p. 17
PAGE 55 *"Brown or white . . . was easy sailing."*: LS, p. 34
PAGE 56 *"Each square foot . . . carousing vermin."*: LS, p. 18
PAGE 60 *"contains history . . . of the world."*: DST, p. 256

CHAPTER 7: The Silent World Below
PAGE 62 *"Soon, perhaps, we . . . to survive."*: LDCS, p. 256
PAGE 64 *"Jacques-Yves Cousteau . . . a poet's feeling."*: TM, February 9, 1953
PAGE 65 *"has been the . . . indispensable tool."*: OIS, p. 119
PAGE 66 *"At fifteen feet . . . virtual black."*: SW. p. 255
PAGE 68 *"They hauled flipping . . . them off."*: LS, p. 134
PAGE 72 *"With no need . . . and pocketbook."*: TM, March 28, 1960

CHAPTER 8: The Conshelf Experiments
PAGE 74 *"It is the first . . . time to see."*: TDP
PAGE 74 *"decided from the . . . jobs might be."*: LS, p. 28
PAGE 74 *"No one shouted . . . a uniform."*: LS, p. 28
PAGE 74 *"discussed plans . . . each other."*: LS, p. 28
PAGE 74 *"supply officer . . . and sonarman."*: LS, p. 29
PAGE 75 *"It completely . . . as 1,150 feet."*: C, p. 58
PAGE 76 *"an escort of . . . ships and docks."*: C, p. 60
PAGE 78 *"It is the first . . . time to see"*: LS, p. 322
PAGE 78 *"obsessed with . . . water comes in?"*: LS, p. 320
PAGE 78 *"decided on a . . . of the settlement."*: WWS, p. 7

CHAPTER 9: A Resident of the Sea
PAGE 84 *"We have been . . . a sewer."*: OIS, P.98
PAGE 85 *"to essentially . . . of the sea."*: C p. 89
PAGE 85 *"You know . . . see dolphins,"*: CCHW
PAGE 87 *"watched and filmed . . . and rituals."*: C, p. 99
PAGE 88 *"It was good . . . overconfident."*: TM, January 19, 1968
PAGE 89 *"We are . . . adventure film."*, NYT, June 26, 1997
PAGE 90 *"certainly bore the . . . Antarctic expedition."*: C, p. 136
PAGE 90 *"end of the world."*
PAGE 90 *"We have been . . . a sewer."*: OIS, p. 98
PAGE 90 *"Monitoring the sea . . . our impact."*: OIS, p. 98
PAGE 91 *"to the protection . . . of the quality of life."*: CCHW, p. 232
PAGE 94 *"samples of water . . . countries."*: C, p. 58
PAGE 95 *"That is fate. . . . move on."*: CCHW, p.181
PAGE 96-97 *"I looked at . . . a better world."*: CCHW, p.182

CHAPTER 10: The Odyssey Continues
PAGE 98 *"To improve the . . . I love it."*: JPC
PAGE 100 *"Our films have . . . an honest observer."*: JPC

CHAPTER 11: The Final Journey Home
PAGE 105 *". . . Captain Cousteau . . . lies within."*: CNN
PAGE 106 *"mother, healer . . . psychiatrist"*: CDNN, March 4, 2003
PAGE 108 *"At my age . . . with pleasure!"*: LAT, November 5, 1995
PAGE 112 *"She's an old . . . a darling."*: NYT, July 15, 1986
PAGE 113 *"Aye Calypso, the . . . you tell."*: John Denver
PAGE 114 *"Through his many . . . human family."*: CNN
PAGE 117 *"When one man . . . to himself."*: CCHW, p. 257

Image Credits

© Authors Image/Alamy: 43
© Photos 12 /Alamy: 67
AP Images: 74, 77, 83, 101, 106
AP Images/Doug Jennings: 117
AP Images/Rene Maestri: 82
AP Images/Dave Pickoff: 92
AP Images/Kathy Willens: 112
Courtesy of Jan Willem Bech: 27, 28
© Corbis: 58
© Tobias Bernhard/zefa/Corbis: 21
© Bettmann/Corbis: 9, 18, 25, 51, 54, 64, 72, 94, 96, 97, 116
© Jonathan Blair/Corbis: 36
© Ralph A. Clevenger.Corbis: 30
© Philippe Eranian/Corbis: 114
© Jack Fields/Corbis: 16
© Stephen Frink/Corbis: 35, 73
© Gallo Images/Corbis: 87
© Todd Gipstein/Corbis: 26
© Hulton-Deutsch Collection/Corbis: 14
© Hekimian Julien/Corbis Sygma: 98
© Wolfgang Kaehler/Corbis: 89
© Matthias Kulka/zefa/Corbis: 41
© Floris Leeuwenberg/The Cover Story/Corbis: 91
© David Lefranc/Kipa/Corbis: 108
© Gail Mooney/Corbis: 49
© Jeffrey L. Rotman/Corbis: 59
© Underwood & Underwood/Corbis: 88
© Ralph White/Corbis: 63
© Lawson Wood/Corbis: 13
Agence France Presse/Getty Images: 86
Fred Ramage/Keystone/Getty Images: 38
RDA/Getty Images: 69

Time Inc./Time Life Pictures/Getty Images: 76
The Granger Collection, New York: 4, 5, 53, 61, 68
Kobal Collection/Picture Desk: 65, 81
Library of Congress: 3, 19, 22, 37, 32, 75, 93, 102
Marine Nationale: 40
Graphic by Jim McMahon: 79
AFP/Newscom: 84
Catala-Roca/Digital Press Photos/Newscom: 45
NOAA: 100
Courtesy of Pandora's Books: 62
Robert Cabane/www.flickr.com: 2
Capt Kim/www.flickr.com: 104
Eco-Index Turismo Sostenible/www.flickr.com: 111
Jose Esteves da Silva/www.flickr.com: 56
Lawrence Lee, September 2007/www.flickr.com: 110
Alain Rolli/www.flickr.com: 113
Jennifer Schmidt/www.flickr.com: 109
Jenn Sinclair/www.flickr.com: 107
Russell Wieland/www.flickr.com: 6
© iStockphoto.com/"Adrian Beesley": 11
© iStockphoto.com/"Michal Besser": 8
© iStockphoto.com/"Christine Gonsalves": 31
Courtesy of www.amazon.com: 105
Courtesy of www.vintagescubasupply.com: 12
Cover art: © Bettmann/Corbis

About the Author

Kathleen Olmstead is a writer and filmmaker who lives in Toronto. As a child, she spent countless—very enjoyable—hours with Jacques Cousteau in his undersea world.

Index

Discover interesting personalities
in the Sterling Biographies® series: